United States
CITIZENSHIP

AGS

by
Michael O'Shea, M.A.

AGS®

American Guidance Service, Inc.
4201 Woodland Road
Circle Pines, MN 55014-1796
1-800-328-2560

Learning About our United States

Printed in the United States of America

ISBN 0–7854–0962–9 (Previously ISBN 0–88671–973–9)

Order Number: 90873

18 V036 12 11

Contents

What Is Citizenship?

 Facts for Citizens

One meaning of *citizen* is "a person who lives in a town or city." A *citizen* is also "a person who has certain rights and privileges."

The word *citizen* comes from the word *city.* This was because people once lived in cities for protection. In those days, a person's **nation** was not as important as it is today.

Today you are a citizen of a city, a county (or parish), a state, and a nation. When we speak of being a citizen, we usually think of the nation of which we are a member. People are citizens of the United States, of Canada, or of some other nation.

Citizenship has two very important meanings. The first meaning of *citizenship* is "a person is a citizen of a nation." A second meaning of *citizenship* has to do with the way people act and live because they are members of a nation.

It is this second meaning of citizenship that will be the focus of this book.

Citizenship gives people certain **rights** in their own nation. When people visit other nations, they may not have all the rights they have at home.

Citizens also have **responsibilities.** Citizenship is a combination of rights and responsibilities. Citizens may not just enjoy their rights. They must also take on the responsibilities of citizenship. Without taking responsibility, it would be impossible to preserve our rights.

 Citizenship at Work

In small groups, discuss the following questions. Write brief answers in the space provided.

1. What do you think are some rights of citizens?

   _____

   _____

2. What do you think are some responsibilities of citizens?

   _____

   _____

Citizenship Documents

A **document** is a written record. There are many written records that are important to citizens.

One of the most important documents is your **birth certificate.** This vital document is the legal record of your birth. It proves you are a citizen of the nation in which you were born. It also gives your date of birth and the names of your parents. This document is so important that it must be kept in a safe place. You need to know exactly where it is kept.

From time to time, you must present an official copy of your birth certificate as **evidence** that you are a citizen of your nation. It also proves that you were born on a certain date. For this reason, many states require young drivers to present a birth certificate in order to apply for their first driver's license.

Not all birth certificates are alike. Some give more information than others. Some are large and fancy. Others are smaller and plain.

Sometimes a birth certificate is lost or destroyed. If this happens, it can be replaced. Copies are kept in the **county** (or **parish) seat** where you were born. The county (or parish) seat is the city in which the county's (or parish's) **government** offices are located.

The **Health Department** for the county (or parish) is usually the place to start if you need a copy of a lost birth certificate.

If you don't have an official copy of your birth certificate or cannot find it, now is the time to get a copy. An official copy has a government seal on it. This document is too important not to have handy.

Another important citizenship document is your **Social Security card.** The card is issued by the United States government. Each social security card has its own Social Security number. This number is used to **identify** you as a specific person. No one else has the same Social Security number as you do.

When you begin a new job, you will be asked for your Social Security number. This important number goes on your tax returns, on credit card applications, on school and college records, and on other important records.

Since a Social Security number is used so often, many people carry their card or at least their number in their purse or wallet.

Your birth certificate and Social Security card are important documents. In many ways they help prove that you are the person you say you are.

Quick Check
Decide whether each statement is true or false. Write *True* or *False* in the space before each statement.

_____ 1. A citizen is a member of a nation.

_____ 2. Your birth certificate proves you are a citizen of your nation.

_____ 3. Citizenship may refer to the way people act.

_____ 4. Documents are written records.

_____ 5. Employers need to know a worker's Social Security number.

_____ 6. Social Security numbers are kept at the health department.

_____ 7. A lost birth certificate cannot be replaced.

_____ 8. You may need your birth certificate to get a driver's license.

_____ 9. A person's date of birth is on his or her birth certificate.

_____ 10. Each person's Social Security number is different.

_____ 11. A Social Security card is a legal record of your birth.

_____ 12. The United States government issues birth certificates.

_____ 13. The names of your parents are listed on your birth certificate.

_____ 14. All birth certificates have the same information.

_____ 15. A birth certificate can be used as evidence of citizenship.

You already know that your birth certificate and Social Security card are important proof that you are a citizen.

Citizenship at Work

There are many facts recorded on your birth certificate. Fill in those facts that you know. If you don't know some of these facts, find your birth certificate and look them up.

1. Your full name as shown on your birth certificate _____

2. The date of your birth _____

3. The city in which you were born _____

4. The state in which you were born _____

5. The country of your birth _____

6. Your parents' full names _____

You probably know where your Social Security card is because you may often need to use your Social Security number.

7. What is your Social Security number? _____

8. Where do you keep your card? _____

9. Does a Social Security card identify your national citizenship? _____

10. Name two forms that ask you to provide your Social Security number.

_____

_____

How You Become a Citizen

 Facts for Citizens

Citizens of a country usually live in that nation. A citizen may visit another country, of course. A person does not give up citizenship in one country even by living in another nation for several years.

Once you are a citizen of your own nation, you usually remain its citizen for your entire life.

The most common way of **acquiring** citizenship, or becoming a citizen, is by being born. If your parents are citizens of a nation, you become a citizen of that same nation at the time of your birth.

What if your parents were living in another nation when you were born? You still become a citizen of the nation your parents called home. However, sometimes a child born in another country becomes a citizen of that nation as well. For instance, if a family moves to Canada from the United States because of a job, the parents are still United States citizens. If, while living in Canada, they have a child, that child is a citizen of the United States. He or she also has the chance to become a citizen of Canada. When this happens, a person has **dual citizenship.** Dual citizenship means that a person is a citizen of two nations.

In this example, the child may have to choose by the age of 18 which citizenship to keep. Once that choice is made, this person will be a citizen of just one nation.

Not all citizens of a nation gained citizenship by being born in that nation. Some people came from other nations and became **naturalized** citizens. They asked permission to enter a nation such as the United States. Once there, they began to study to become citizens.

Naturalized citizens have almost all the rights and responsibilities of a citizen born in that country. Any person living in a country who is not a citizen is an **alien.** An alien is a person from another nation who has not yet become a citizen of the nation in which he or she now lives.

Some aliens are **legal aliens.** They have permission to be in a nation of which they are not citizens. Tourists, certain workers, and legal immigrants are legal aliens.

Other aliens are **illegal aliens.** They do not have permission to be in a nation. These people have sneaked into the country. If they are discovered, they will be arrested and **deported.** Being deported means being sent back to the country where one is a citizen.

Until just recently it was very hard for an illegal alien to become a United States citizen. In 1986, laws were passed that made it possible for many illegal aliens then in the United States to become legal aliens. Once they became legal aliens, they could one day become citizens of the United States if they wanted to. These laws are no longer in effect.

Many people visit other nations. In order to do this, they must apply for a **passport.** Governments issue passports to travelers. A passport is a little book containing your name, birth date, and place of birth. It tells whether you are male or female, identifies your national citizenship, and contains your photograph and **signature.** It tells when you got your passport and when it will **expire,** or no longer be good.

Quick Check
Write *True* or *False* in the space before each statement.

_____ **1.** All aliens are illegal aliens.

_____ **2.** A person does not become a citizen until one year of age.

_____ **3.** A passport proves that a person is a citizen of his or her nation.

_____ **4.** Each person needs to sign his or her passport.

_____ **5.** Most people become citizens of the nation in which they were born.

_____ **6.** Naturalized citizens must first be illegal aliens.

_____ **7.** Aliens are not citizens of any nation.

_____ **8.** A tourist in another nation is an illegal alien.

_____ **9.** A legal alien is a person who has permission to be in a foreign country.

_____ **10.** You are <u>not</u> a citizen of the United States if you were born to American citizens living in a foreign country.

Citizenship Begins at Home

 Facts for Citizens

Citizenship involves a combination of **rights** and **responsibilities**. This is true at home just as it is true in the city or town in which you live. You are a citizen of your home as well as your nation.

Members of a **family** have certain rights. A right is something to which a person is entitled. The rights of family members are the result of being a member of that family. These rights are due to your birth.

Some children join families by **adoption.** Adoption is a **legal** method of making one or more children members of a family. Adopted children have the same family rights as children who are members by birth.

Just as members of a family have rights, they also have responsibilities. A responsibility is something that is required of you. It is something you need to do if your family is to function properly.

Children have the *right* to be considered members of their family. Members of a family have the *responsibility* to treat each other properly.

Think of a responsibility as a burden. A burden is something that has to be carried. So is a responsibility. It may be **moral** responsibility that you *feel* you must take care of. A responsibility may be a **legal** burden. If this is the case, there is a law *requiring* you to take care of the responsibility.

Responsibilities are **obligations** that good citizens must bear. This is true in the family and in larger groups such as a school, a city, or a nation.

We call these larger groups **society.** You have responsibilities to society just as you do to your own family. In fact, your family is part of society. It is the first social institution you belong to. A **social institution** is a system of social organization. You depend on your family for many things, including **basic needs** such as food, clothing, and shelter. Your family can also give you a sense of belonging and of feeling safe.

U N I T 1

Quick Check

Use one of the terms from the list below to complete each sentence.

adoption	legal	right	basic
family	society	responsibility	organization

1. An obligation, or something required, is a _____.

2. An _____ is a legal way of making a child part of a new family.

3. Something to which a person is entitled is a _____.

4. A group of related people is known as a _____ and is part of society.

5. Something done according to the law is called _____.

6. Many people living together, following similar laws, is a _____.

7. A social institution is a system of social _____.

8. The first social institution people belong to is the _____.

9. Members of a family have a _____ to treat each other properly.

10. Needs such as food and clothing are called _____ needs.

For most of us, **school** is the first place we get to practice citizenship outside our home. School is far larger than our home in size and in the number of people involved. As **students,** we have rights and responsibilities that are more complicated than those in our home.

Perhaps the most important **right** we have as students is the right to a **free public** education. This means that every citizen of our nation has the right to go to school. Not only may children go to school, but they also have the right to attend school without having to pay. This means those who pay **taxes** are paying for the cost of education for all students in public schools.

As a student, you also have these personal rights:

- You have the right to expect your teachers to be well educated and able to teach properly.

- You have the right to be safe at school from **physical harm**.

- You have the right to be treated with respect.

As a student and member of your school, you also have many responsibilities.

- You have the responsibility of treating other students and teachers with respect.

- You also have the responsibility of helping make others safe and of respecting the possessions of others.

- Perhaps most important of all, you have the responsibility to do your best. You are responsible for trying to learn what your teachers try to teach you.

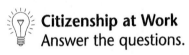 **Citizenship at Work**
Answer the questions.

1. Which right related to school is most important to you?

_____

_____

_____

2. Which responsibility related to school is most important to you?

_____

_____

3. How do your rights affect teachers?

_____

_____

4. How do teachers' rights affect you?

_____

_____

Facts for Citizens

Many of our rights are based on the Constitution of the United States. The Constitution tells how our government is set up. It is our plan of government. It also tells what powers our government has and what rights we have as citizens.

(A special part of the Constitution, called the **Bill of Rights,** is so important we will study it separately a little later on.)

We often hear people speak of their **constitutional rights.** What they are saying is that they feel they have the right to do something because of our Constitution.

At other times, someone may say that an action is **unconstitutional.** This simply means that the person thinks something goes against what the Constitution says.

Have you ever considered how strange it would be if the citizens of one state had **basic rights** different from those of people who lived in another state? Our Constitution says every state and every citizen has to be treated the same by our government.

Of course, one state can have a **law** that another state does not have. States have the right under the Constitution to pass laws that apply to their citizens.

However, no state or city or town can pass laws that go against the Constitution. If such a law is passed, it is up to the **courts** to tell the state or city that the law is wrong.

Let's take a quick look at some of our rights as citizens that are **guaranteed** by the Constitution.

Was a law passed by the United States **Congress** that you don't like? Citizens over the age of 18 have the right to vote in the next **election** against the people who made the law.

Do you and your family want to take a trip to another state? Are you thinking of moving to another city or state? You have the right to travel from state to state for any **lawful** reason.

While on a trip, you may want to buy something. You have the right to pay for it in United States money, no matter which state you are in.

Do you want a job? You have the right to work, provided you have the proper **qualifications** for that job. This means that you can show you have enough education, skills, and experience to do the work properly.

Are you sick? As a citizen, you have the right to expect the doctor who treats you to have the proper education.

Do the police suspect you of doing something wrong? As a citizen, you have the right to proper treatment when you are **arrested** and after your arrest.

Here is a quick summary of your rights as a citizen: you have the right to do anything you wish, as long as it does not break the law or harm other citizens. That should be easy to remember.

Quick Check

Mark each statement below either *True* or *False*.

_____ 1. Something that goes against the Constitution is unconstitutional.

_____ 2. Voters have the right to vote against lawmakers who pass laws the citizens do not like.

_____ 3. If a law is passed that does not agree with the Constitution, there is nothing that can be done about it.

_____ 4. A state can pass a law for its citizens even if the law goes against the Constitution.

_____ 5. The Constitution is our plan of government.

_____ 6. Citizens must be over the age of 25 to vote.

_____ 7. Citizens of one state cannot move to another state unless they get permission.

_____ 8. You can pay for goods with United States money in Hawaii.

_____ 9. You have the right to work at a job even if you do not have the qualifications for the job.

_____ 10. You have the right to do anything you want as long as what you do does not break a law or harm others.

Facts for Citizens

We have already learned that citizenship involves certain **responsibilities**. Responsibilities are duties or obligations. All citizens must share in citizenship responsibilities. Unless we all carry our share of responsibilities, some of our citizenship rights may be lost.

A basic responsibility of citizens is to obey the **law.** If citizens do not obey the law and show **respect** for it, many people suffer.

When we speak of the law, we are talking about all the laws that affect our lives. These laws are passed by all **levels of government.** In the United States, we have **local** government, which is our town or city **council.** We also have state laws passed, or **enacted,** by our state government. Of course, we have **federal** laws passed by **Congress,** which meets in Washington, D. C.

Laws are rules for living. They are made so that citizens of a nation know what to expect and how they must act. When laws are broken, someone is harmed. When someone is hurt by the ways others act, that person has lost some of his or her rights as a citizen.

Washington. D.C.

Citizens don't always think that certain laws are right. No matter how we feel, we still must obey the laws. Obeying the laws of our nation is just one of the responsibilities of being citizens.

If citizens feel a law is wrong or that it harms citizens, then they may work to have the law changed. Not only do citizens have the right to ask that a law be changed, they also have a responsibility to do this. As we have already discussed, citizens may vote against lawmakers who pass laws that people do not believe are right.

Citizens also have the responsibility to let their lawmakers know why a law is bad. Citizens must take the responsibility of telling lawmakers which laws are good or bad. Then there is a better chance that lawmakers will not pass improper laws.

In an earlier lesson, we discovered that citizens have the right to **vote** for or against the people who make laws. **Voting** is a responsibility as well as a right.

When citizens do not take on the responsibilities that are their duties, government may not function as effectively as it might. We have the right to have good **government**. Therefore, we must take the responsibility of choosing good people for government.

We all have the right to **protection** for ourselves and for our property. This is why we have police and fire departments and the **military,** or armed forces. We also have the responsibility to help these people protect us.

It is the duty of citizens not only to obey the law, but also to help law officers do their duty. Good citizens get **involved.** They **report** crimes that they know about. They are willing to tell law officers what they have seen. This is a necessary part of taking on the responsibilities of citizenship.

Citizens have rights when they are **accused** of crimes. Citizens also have the responsibility of being part of a **jury** when others are on **trial** for a crime. If people will not serve on juries, others may lose the right to be judged by their peers.

Citizens have the right to services that the government provides. Government builds roads, runs schools, and maintains roads and sewers. As citizens, it is our responsibility to pay taxes so that government will have the money to provide these services. As you can see, rights and responsibilities of citizenship are tied together. To keep our rights, we must accept our responsibilities.

Fill each blank below with the correct word. The answers are all written in bold type on the pages you just read.

1. Citizens must _____ for the best people if our government is going to be as good as it should be.

2. Another name for the army, navy, and air force that help protect us is the

   _____.

3. When citizens take responsibility for helping our law officers, these citizens are

   getting _____.

4. Laws that affect the entire nation are those passed by _____.

5. When a city _____ passes a law, that law applies just to citizens of that town or city.

6. Good citizenship means people must obey and respect the

   _____.

7. When a law is passed, it is _____.

8. When police or other law officers think a person has committed a crime, that

   person is _____ of the crime.

9. One of the rights of a citizen is to a fair _____ if he or she is accused of a crime.

10. Laws are passed by many _____ of government, such as local, state, and federal.

11. _____ is a responsibility as well as a right.

12. We all have the right to _____ from physical harm.

Losing Citizenship Rights

 Facts for Citizens

You know that citizenship provides certain rights for citizens. With these rights come responsibilities. When citizens do not live up to their responsibilities, they may lose some of their rights.

Voting is both a right and a responsibility. It is an extremely important right that can be lost.

In order to vote, a citizen must first **register.** This simply means giving one's name and address to the **county clerk.** Voters must be at least 18 years old to register.

A citizen who does not register may not vote. Millions of citizens in the United States do not register. Thus, they lose their right to vote for those who will **govern** them. By not voting, people lose the right to have much to say about who will make the rules by which we live.

Citizens who commit **crimes** lose many of their rights as part of their punishment. Most important is their loss of freedom to move from place to place. Also, those **convicted** of certain crimes lose the privilege of choosing certain jobs, voting, getting some kinds of licenses, and holding some public offices.

It is even possible for a citizen to lose his or her **citizenship.** One way to do this is to try to **overthrow** the government. A person who is convicted of trying to harm our government is guilty of **treason.** A citizen convicted of treason may end up without citizenship.

Voting in an **election** in a **foreign** nation is another way people may lose United States citizenship. Anyone who serves in a foreign army without permission of the United States government may lose his or her citizenship.

A member of the United States **military** who **deserts** may also lose citizenship. A military member who deserts runs away or leaves his or her military responsibilities.

It is even easier for a **naturalized** citizen to lose his or her citizenship. If a naturalized citizen lies during the naturalization hearings, his or her citizenship can be taken away.

If a naturalized citizen leaves the United States to live in a foreign country within a few years of gaining United States citizenship, he or she may lose citizenship.

The easiest way to lose one's rights and privileges as a citizen is not to live up to the responsibilities of citizenship.

Every time a citizen fails to be responsible, some rights are lost. The citizen who commits crimes takes away rights from others. A citizen who does not take an interest in our government loses the right to expect the government to do what he or she wants.

What it all comes down to is this: when citizens do not live up to their responsibilities, some of their rights and privileges are lost.

Quick Check
Fill each blank with one of the **bold** words in this lesson.

1. The crime of trying to overthrow our government is _____.

2. A member of the armed forces who leaves or runs away is one who _____.

3. By voting, citizens choose who will _____ them.

4. In order to vote, a citizen must first _____.

5. When someone is _____ of a crime, he or she is found guilty.

6. _____ are committed when laws are broken.

7. An _____ is held so that citizens may vote to decide who will hold certain public offices.

8. A person registers to vote by providing information to the _____.

9. A _____ citizen can lose his or her citizenship if the government discovers that the person lied during citizenship hearings.

10. American citizens cannot vote in an election in a _____ country.

Review Unit 1

■ Choose the term from the list that matches each definition.

adoption	Constitution	military	right
alien	council	naturalized	society
applicant	document	offense	treason
birth certificate	family	passport	
Congress	law	responsibility	

_____ 1. A written record

_____ 2. The small group in which most of us learn about citizenship

_____ 3. Document that proves we were born at a certain time and place

_____ 4. Document used by travelers to prove they are citizens of their nation

_____ 5. Citizens who are not born in the nation in which they are now citizens

_____ 6. A person living in a nation of which he or she is not a citizen

_____ 7. One who applies or asks for a document

_____ 8. A crime or wrongdoing

_____ 9. Word meaning all the people living together in a nation

_____ 10. A crime against our government

_____ 11. Our armed forces

_____ 12. The document that is the basis of many of our rights

_____ 13. A duty or obligation

_____ 14. A rule passed by the government

_____ 15. The lawmaking group that runs a town or city

_____ 16. The lawmaking group that makes laws for the United States

_____ 17. A legal way of making a child part of a new family

_____ 18. A privilege that belongs to a citizen

The Constitution

The Constitution is sometimes called the Supreme Law of the Land. What this means is that every law passed in the nation is supposed to agree with the Constitution. Any law **enacted** by a state or city cannot disagree with anything said in the Constitution. Any law that does not agree with the Constitution is **unconstitutional.** Such a law will eventually be brought to a **court.** When a court says a law goes against the Constitution, that law is no longer a law.

More than two hundred years ago, state representatives met in Philadelphia to attend a constitutional convention. They discussed many ideas. Finally, they wrote the Constitution of the United States. They wrote it as a plan for our government. It explained how the government at the national level would be organized.

The Constitution opens with a **preamble,** or introduction. The preamble lists the reasons for the new Constitution. These reasons are to form a better union, or central government; to establish justice for all; to make sure American society stays peaceful; to defend the nation; to promote good conditions for all Americans; and to make sure the country will always be free.

The Constitution is divided into several parts. Each of these parts is called an **Article.** Each article in the Constitution deals with one specific area of our government.

For instance, Article I deals with **Congress.** It tells us about the **Senate** and the **House of Representatives.** This article states who may become a **senator** or a **representative.** It also tells how these people may be elected and how long they will **hold office.** The same article also tells us what Congress can and cannot do.

Article II covers the **President.** It tells who may be elected to this high office and how the election will be held. Just as the first article identifies the powers of Congress, the second article tells us what **powers** or authority our President has.

The third Article tells how our court system is set up. It also provides for a **Supreme Court.** This court is the highest court in the land. It is the Supreme Court that decides whether a law agrees with the Constitution. The Supreme Court also decides whether or not a **lower court** has made a correct decision. In cases in which two or more states have a disagreement, the Supreme Court can be called upon to settle the argument.

Article IV says that the citizens of each state will be treated the same. This gives citizens the same rights and responsibilities regardless of where they live. It also says that a person cannot avoid being punished for a crime by moving from one state to another. This article tells how new states may be added to the United States. (Remember that when the Constitution was written, there were only thirteen states in the new nation.)

The people who wrote the Constitution knew that in the years to come changes might have to be made. For that reason, they added Article V, which tells how to change, or **amend**, the Constitution. In the next lesson you will learn about some of the Constitutional changes, or **amendments.**

Article VI is very short, but quite important. One of the most important things in the Constitution is in this article. Here it says that the Constitution and laws passed by Congress are the **Supreme Law of the Land.** No laws passed by states or other local governments may change what the Constitution says or what United States laws say.

The final article tells how the Constitution is to be accepted by the states. This is called **ratification.** To go into effect, 9 out of the 13 states had to approve the Constitution. In June 1788, New Hampshire became the ninth state to approve it. The Constitution then took effect. Within two years, all 13 original states approved the Constitution.

Let's look at several actual paragraphs from the Constitution. Each is written in very formal language.

 Citizenship at Work
Answer each of these questions either *Yes* or *No.*

The first paragraph comes from Article I, Section 2.

No person shall be a representative who shall not have attained to the age of twenty-five years, and been seven years a citizen of the United States, and who shall not, when elected, be an inhabitant of that state in which he shall be chosen.

1. Ms. Browne lives in New York. Can she be elected to represent people from Virginia?

   _____

2. Mr. Chavez was born in Mexico but is a naturalized citizen of the United States.

   Can he become a representative? _____

3. Ms. Johnson is 38 years old. Can she serve as a member of the House

   of Representatives? _____

4. Mr. Miller was born in England 29 years ago. He became a naturalized citizen of the United States four years ago. Can he now be elected to the House of Representatives? _____

This paragraph comes from Section 1 of Article 2.

No person except a natural-born citizen or a citizen of the United States at the time of the adoption of this Constitution shall be eligible to the office of President; neither shall any person be eligible to that office who shall not have attained the age of thirty-five years and been fourteen years a resident within the United States.

5. Sylvia Perez was born in Mexico and came to the United States as a young girl. She became a citizen over 14 years ago. Can Sylvia become President? _____

6. Kareem abu Sim was born in the United States, has never visited a foreign country, and will be 35 years old a month after the presidential election. Can Kareem become President if elected? _____

7. John Mordini is a 40-year-old American citizen born in the United States. He worked in Japan for eight years, but he returned to the United States four years ago. Can he run for President this year? _____

Here is Section 2 of Article IV.

The citizens of each state shall be entitled to all privileges and immunities of citizens in the several states.

8. A person in Illinois has the right to own a home. Can that person move to Texas and still have the right to buy a home? _____

9. When a person is arrested in Montana, he or she has the right to call a lawyer. Do people living in Oregon have that same right? _____

Facts for Citizens

When the Constitution was written, people realized changes would have to be made later on to meet the needs of people in the future.

For this reason, the writers made it possible to **amend,** or change, the Constitution. The first ten changes, or **amendments,** were known as the **Bill of Rights.**

Let's take a look at some of the freedoms, or **liberties,** we enjoy because of the Bill of Rights.

The First Amendment says that Congress cannot pass any laws that keep citizens from **worshiping** as they please or from not worshiping at all if they wish.

The same amendment also says citizens have the right to **freedom of speech.** This means, as citizens, we can speak our minds. It does not mean we can say things that are not true about other people. We also cannot use words that present "clear and present danger." For example, we cannot shout "Fire!" in a crowded theater when there isn't any fire.

Also in the First Amendment is our guarantee for freedom of the **press.** Our government is not allowed to stop newspapers from printing the truth.

One of the freedoms in this same amendment is one that we often do not think about, but that is extremely important. This is the freedom of peaceful **assembly.** This allows citizens to hold peaceful meetings to discuss problems and talk about new ideas.

Another important guarantee in the First Amendment is the right to petition the government to correct injustices. This means that citizens may ask the government to handle their complaints about the government. They may ask the government to find solutions to the problems they identify.

The Second Amendment says that people have the right to keep arms for the purpose of maintaining a state militia. Congress has passed laws against the ownership of some types of firearms. For example, citizens may not own certain types of semi-automatic weapons.

The Third Amendment states that in peacetime, people cannot be forced to give soldiers a place to live in their homes. They also cannot be forced to do so during wartime, except as provided for by law.

The Fourth Amendment states that citizens are safe from unreasonable **searches and seizures.** What this means is that, unless there is a good reason for police or other law officers to search your home or car or business, they cannot do so. In order to search your property, they must first get permission from a court. This permission is called a **search warrant.**

The Fourth Amendment also says that police or courts may not seize things you own without proper reasons. This keeps an officer from coming into your home or business and taking things that belong to you when there is no legal reason for doing so.

In the Fifth Amendment, citizens are given **protections** when they are accused of crimes. A citizen cannot be charged with murder or another major crime unless members of a grand jury say so. A **grand jury**, with twenty-three members, is about twice the size of a regular jury. The grand jury listens to the **evidence** and decides whether or not a person should be charged with the crime.

This same amendment states that a person cannot be put on **trial** twice for the same crime if that person had been found "not guilty." An accused person does not have to answer questions in court if the answers might help prove him or her guilty.

Also included in the Fifth Amendment is freedom from having **private property** taken away by the government unless it is paid for.

The Sixth Amendment says that a citizen accused of a crime has a right to a jury trial. Also, the person must be told what charges he or she is accused of. This amendment gives the accused the right to an attorney and to call in witnesses to support his or her position.

The Seventh Amendment gives citizens the right to ask for a jury trial in civil cases that involve more than $20. A civil case is a lawsuit.

The Eighth Amendment prohibits very high bails for people accused of crimes. Bail is money given by the accused as a guarantee that he or she will appear for trial. The court returns the money if the accused does appear. The amendment also prohibits cruel or unusual punishments for persons found guilty of crimes.

The Ninth Amendment says that the Constitution does not list all of the rights of the people. They have other rights besides those named in the Constitution.

The Tenth Amendment is extremely important. It says that unless the Constitution gives a certain power to the **federal** government, that power or right belongs to the states or to the people. This helps guarantee that our government in Washington will not become more powerful than it should.

Citizenship at Work

Mark with an X next to each of the ideas below that the Bill of Rights gives to citizens of the United States.

_____ 1. Citizens may go to any church they wish.

_____ 2. American citizens do not have to attend church unless they want to do so.

_____ 3. Police may not search your home unless they have a legal reason to do so.

_____ 4. A person accused of a crime has the right to have a jury trial.

_____ 5. Newspaper writers may write anything they wish, whether or not it is true, because they have freedom of the press.

_____ 6. So long as we tell the truth, we are allowed to say what we wish even if we criticize our government.

_____ 7. A judge may have a person brought to trial without telling him or her what the criminal charge is.

_____ 8. Citizens may hold a meeting to discuss what they feel is wrong with their government.

_____ 9. A grand jury must decide whether or not the police have enough evidence to charge a person with a crime such as murder.

_____ 10. The states and private citizens have any rights that the Constitution does not give to the federal government.

_____ 11. A person charged with a crime must answer all questions asked of him or her in court no matter what the questions are.

_____ 12. Once a person is found innocent of a crime, he or she may not be tried again for the same crime.

_____ 13. People must give soldiers room and board in their homes.

_____ 14. Only defendants in a criminal trial have the right to be tried by a jury.

_____ 15. Cruel and unusual punishment is forbidden.

Facts for Citizens

The Bill of Rights provides many personal freedoms for citizens of our nation. According to our Constitution, these freedoms may not be taken away from citizens.

One of our most important freedoms is the freedom of **speech.** Being able to say what you wish is one of the many freedoms we have as citizens of the United States.

Sometimes citizens abuse this freedom. Being allowed to say what we wish is not the same as saying something that is not true. Telling lies or saying things we know will hurt others is not part of our freedom of speech. Saying something false about another person is an **abuse** of freedom of speech. A lie is a **violation** of our freedom to speak freely.

Freedom of the **press** is another important freedom that is sometimes abused. **Newspapers** must be allowed to print the truth freely. This is one way of keeping all citizens **informed.**

When a newspaper reporter or editor writes a news story without checking the **facts,** freedom of the press is abused.

In the United States, we have the freedom to **worship** as we please. We also have the right not to take part in any religion. Many of the first European settlers came here to have **religious** freedom.

It is not uncommon for members of one religious **faith** or group to say bad things about other religions. In some places, workers who do not belong to a certain church find it hard to get a job. Even though the Constitution says this is wrong, it does happen. Any time a person is discriminated against because of his or her religion, our freedom to worship as we please is abused.

Another important freedom that is sometimes abused is the freedom of **assembly.** Part of our way of life is to be able to meet with friends to discuss things. What would happen to our way of life if we were not allowed to have parties, picnics, or dances? How would citizens feel if we were told we could no longer attend concerts, ball games, plays, or political rallies?

Even though freedom to assemble peacefully is a most important freedom, it is one that can be abused. When a party in the city park turns into a gang fight, those involved have abused a freedom. When fans at a ball game begin throwing things onto the playing field, they are violating the rights of others around them. A rock concert that ends in a street riot is certainly an abuse of freedom of assembly.

Each time anyone violates our basic freedoms, he or she is hurting others. When a citizen abuses his or her privileges, someone else is losing a little bit of freedom.

 Citizenship at Work
Read each statement below. Decide which right or freedom is involved. Write the letter of that right or freedom in the space given. You may use some letters more than once.

a. Freedom of speech
b. Freedom of the press
c. Freedom of religion
d. Freedom to assemble
e. Freedom from illegal search and seizure
f. Right to jury trial
g. Right to a speedy trial
h. Right to bail
i. Right to reasonable fines if convicted

j. Freedom from unusual or cruel punishment
k. Freedom from having to board soldiers
l. Right to an attorney
m. Right to complain to the government and ask for changes
n. Right to call witnesses to testify for you

_____ 1. Stella was arrested for shoplifting. She was told her case would be taken to court for trial in about six weeks.

_____ 2. To prevent drugs from coming into the city, the police began stopping drivers and searching their cars for illegal drugs.

_____ 3. A police officer stopped Tom for driving recklessly. Tom said this was not true and wanted his fellow citizens to decide whether he was guilty or not.

_____ 4. The local newspaper carried a story about a successful businessperson who had cheated some workers by taking their retirement payments.

_____ 5. In Rosita's town, nearly everybody belonged to one church. Her church was very small and was attended by only about a hundred worshipers.

_____ 6. Lucinda was a candidate for political office. Her opponent was telling lies about her in his speeches.

_____ 7. After Bob was arrested, he was able to leave jail in a few hours. He deposited $500 to guarantee that he would appear at his court hearing.

_____ 8. The Political Club at Lin's school met to decide which of the people running for town council were the best candidates for the office.

_____ 9. One of Larry's friends was arrested for theft. The next day police officers came to Larry's house without a warrant and asked to look at his room.

_____ 10. The judge found Marilyn guilty of speeding and fined her $30 plus another $10 for court costs.

_____ 11. The Shermans refused to allow soldiers to live in their home.

_____ 12. Many people did not like the new law passed by Congress. Some signed petitions asking Congress to change the law.

_____ 13. Aaron was found guilty of trespassing on a celebrity's property. The judge sentenced him to three years in jail and to wearing a sign admitting his crime for the rest of his life.

_____ 14. Sandy was being tried for a crime committed on September 4, 1996. She wanted her husband to tell the court that they were out of town that day, so Sandy could not have committed the crime. The judge said that her husband could not testify in court.

_____ 15. After his arrest, Avery hired a lawyer to represent him during his trial.

_____ 16. Terrell was escorted off an airplane and taken into custody after making a joke about hijacking.

Other Amendments to the Constitution

 Facts for Citizens

After the Bill of Rights became part of the Constitution, only two new amendments were added in the next seventy years. There are now twenty-seven amendments.

Let's look at some of the amendments that were added between the time the Civil War ended and today.

The Thirteenth Amendment states that there shall be no more **slavery** in our nation. This amendment does allow **convicted** criminals to be put in prison. Prison is a punishment and is not slavery.

In the Fourteenth Amendment, states were told they could not pass laws that would take life, **liberty,** or property from people except according to the law. This amendment also gave voting rights to African American men. It said that the number of **Representatives** elected by a state depended upon the state's population. It also said that the population used to determine the number of representatives would be lowered by the same number of people a state prevented from voting. This part of the amendment was never enforced.

The Fifteenth Amendment made it against the law for a state to keep people from voting because of their race or color or because they were once slaves.

We pay **income taxes** today because of the Sixteenth Amendment. That amendment became law in 1913 and allowed the government to collect taxes on income.

The Seventeenth Amendment changed the way senators were elected. With this amendment, citizens voted directly for senators.

Six years later, the Eighteenth Amendment was added. It **prohibited** making or selling alcoholic drinks. In 1933, the Twenty-first Amendment **repealed** this law and said it was again legal to make and sell alcoholic drinks.

In 1920, the Nineteenth Amendment gave women the right to **vote.**

By 1951, many people were afraid we might someday have a President who was elected to office too many times. The Twenty-second Amendment says that no person may be elected President more than twice. It also said that, if a Vice-President became President and served for more than two years of someone else's **term,** then that person could be elected only once as President.

The Twenty-fourth Amendment outlawed poll taxes. Some states had passed laws saying people could not vote unless they paid a tax. This amendment made those laws unconstitutional.

The Twenty-fifth Amendment set up a system for replacing a President who became unable to finish his or her term of office due to illness. The same amendment allowed the President to **nominate** a new Vice-President, if the Vice-President died or left office.

For many years, people said that if citizens were old enough to go to war, they were old enough to vote. Finally, in 1971, the Twenty-sixth Amendment allowed men and women 18 years of age to vote.

You noticed, of course, that we did not talk about all the amendments that have been passed since the Bill of Rights. Most encyclopedias and *The World Almanac* have copies of the Constitution. Why not look up the rest of the amendments and see what changes were made?

 Quick Check
Write the number of the amendment that allowed each thing to happen.

_____ 1. After the Civil War ended, the Green family members were made free. They were no longer slaves belonging to a plantation owner in Georgia.

_____ 2. By April 15 of each year, millions of Americans must fill out their income tax returns and mail them to the Internal Revenue Service.

_____ 3. In 1921, Mr. Lee was arrested for selling beer.

_____ 4. When Mrs. Henderson voted in 1922, she was the first woman in her family to enter an election booth.

_____ 5. If some future President suffers a stroke that makes it impossible for him or her to speak or move, the Vice-President will be able to become our new leader.

_____ 6. At no time now or in the future can a person serve for more than two terms as President.

_____ 7. When Linda was eighteen-and-a-half years old, she voted in an election.

_____ 8. Peter can vote without having to pay a poll tax.

_____ 9. All senators are elected by voters in their states.

_____ 10. This amendment repealed the Eighteenth Amendment.

Review Unit 2

Choose the word that best completes each sentence. All answers were written in **bold** in the lessons you just studied.

1. Freedom of religion gives us the right of _____ as we wish.

2. Freedom of _____ gives citizens the right to speak as they wish.

3. The Constitution is divided into seven parts, and each part is called an _____.

4. The Thirteenth Amendment freed those who had been in _____.

5. The highest court in the United States is the _____.

6. Without freedom of the _____, our newspapers would lose much of their value.

7. Another name for freedom is _____.

8. Article I of the Constitution tells about our _____, which makes laws for the nation.

9. Freedom from illegal _____ and seizures helps keep our homes safe.

10. All laws in the United States must agree with the _____.

11. The right to get together peacefully is the right of _____.

12. People accused of crimes are entitled to a _____ by jury.

13. Along with the House of Representatives, the _____ makes up our Congress.

14. Our _____ may now be elected to only two terms in office.

15. The government in Washington, D. C., that makes laws for the entire nation is called our _____ government.

16. The _____ identifies some of the freedoms citizens have.

17. Changes to the Constitution are called _____.

18. The Constitution begins with the _____.

19. The Sixteenth Amendment made it possible for the government to collect _____.

20. The Constitution is also called _____ of the land.

Attitudes of Good Citizens

 Facts for Citizens

When he became President of the United States in 1960, John F. Kennedy made this statement famous. He said, "Ask not what your country can do for you; ask what you can do for your country."

President Kennedy was not the first person to say these words. Since then, the words he spoke have been repeated many times. They sum up nicely the sort of **attitude** a good citizen should have.

An attitude, of course, is a way of thinking. The citizenship attitudes we are interested in studying about are those that deal with the rights and responsibilities of good citizens.

One of the worst attitudes a citizen can have is being **selfish.** A great many of our rights and **freedoms** exist only because most people are not selfish. Let us see how selfishness can hurt rights and privileges.

We have to have people who give their time and energy to make the nation a better place in which to live. Someone has to run for public office. Someone has to offer his or her time to serve on the **school board,** the **library board,** the **water board,** and all the other groups that help keep our schools and cities running.

Good citizens have to realize that every citizen is **entitled** to certain rights. When any one person tries to have only rights and no responsibilities, other people have to accept those responsibilities. Not accepting one's responsibilities as a citizen is a way of being selfish.

Instead of always saying what is wrong with our nation, citizens need to try to learn how to make the country better. It is easier to find fault than to find a way to solve problems. As citizens, we have the right to **criticize** and tell others what needs to be changed. At the same time, we also have the responsibility to look for a way to make things better.

A caring society needs people willing to help others. Sometimes helping others means using some of our own freedoms.

For example, we have freedom of speech and of assembly. When meetings are held to discuss community problems, we can often help others by going to the meeting. Once there, we can say what we think about problems. Only when we let others know our **opinions** and ideas can we begin to help solve problems.

Sometimes citizens have to be willing to give up some things for the good of their country. They also have to be willing to take responsibility for trying to make the nation a better place in which to live.

 Citizenship at Work
Decide whether the individuals in each situation show a good attitude or a poor attitude. Write *Good* or *Poor* in the spaces given.

SITUATION 1

Juanita complained time and time again about the way the school dance committee ran the dances. She thought the dances could be better organized. She also thought there should be a greater variety of music.

"Why do you complain all the time?" her mother asked. "Why not do something about it?"

Juanita thought this over and decided she would do something. When the next dance was planned, Juanita was part of the committee. _____

SITUATION 2

Tony was tired of seeing all the trash that students threw away that could be recycled. He thought it was a waste of resources to throw away paper, cans, and bottles that could be recycled.

"Something needs to be done," Tony said.

He talked to his student council representative about the problem. She asked Tony for suggestions.

"For a start, how about putting recycling containers in the classrooms and the cafeteria and on the playground?" Tony suggested. "After all, if the recycling containers are there, maybe more people will use them." _____

SITUATION 3

"I hate income tax time," Joan groaned. "The income tax form does not make sense. Besides, it is not fair for the government to take away money I make so that it can be used to build a highway in another state."

"I know a way to keep from having to pay so much tax," Lois said.

"What's that?" Joan was interested.

"Well, to begin with, you claimed the money you made baby-sitting. The people paid you in cash, so there is no way for the government to know about it. If you claim only what you made at Quik Foods, you won't have to pay much tax at all."

_____

SITUATION 4

Marietta moaned, "Oh, no, I got a D on my test. That will lower my average to a C-. Now I won't be able to play on the varsity volleyball team because my grade average is below a C."

"Didn't you study for the test?" LaShana asked.

"Not really," Marietta replied. "Everyone knows that key varsity players are always given passing grades. I'm going to complain to the coach and see what she can do about the grade."

"Why don't you ask the math teacher if there is something you can do to raise your grade?" asked LaShana. "Maybe she will let you do extra work or take a makeup test."

"Are you kidding? Why should I do makeup work if the coach can help me get my grade changed?" Marietta answered.

_____

SITUATION 5

"Can you believe it? I finally get my license, and my dad says I can take the family car to school. What happens? The school will issue parking passes only to seniors. That means only seniors can park in the school lots. There's no other place in the area to park, so because I'm a junior, I can't drive to school. I still have to take the bus," complained Pedro.

"It doesn't seem fair, does it?" Ariana answered. "But what can we do?"

"I have an idea," Ross offered. "We could draw up a petition and ask sophomores and juniors who drive to sign it. We could then present our petition to the school board. Maybe the board will reconsider the parking situation."

"Good idea!" Ariana and Pedro agreed. "Let's get started now."

_____

Facts for Citizens

In the last lesson, we discussed some of the attitudes that good citizens have. One of the attitudes required of good citizens is a willingness to **get involved.** There are many different ways that citizens can get involved. Following are just a few of the ways that citizens do get involved.

When we talk about getting involved, one of the first things that often comes to mind is getting involved in **law enforcement.** The police and other law officers often ask citizens to become involved by reporting crimes or suspected crimes. This helps them do their jobs and better protect honest citizens.

Just by **obeying** the law and doing nothing to harm others, we are also involved with law enforcement. When good citizens do their part, they are involved citizens.

While we are talking about the law, have you ever stopped to think that by serving on a **jury,** a citizen is involved in **preserving** rights for others?

There are many **service** groups and clubs that do things to help citizens. These organizations often take part in **civic projects** that help make their town or city a better place to live.

You don't have to join one of these groups to get involved in projects that help your **community.** School classes and clubs, student councils, and sports groups often take part in projects that will help the people in their town or city.

Not all groups work to raise money for projects. Many groups get involved as good citizens by **donating** their time and energy. By giving their time, people often provide things that money alone cannot **buy.**

When citizens vote, they are getting involved. Taking part in choosing who will **represent** us is a very important part of being involved.

Even before **election** time, good citizens become involved. They do this by reading all they can about the people running for public office. They attend meetings and listen to the **candidates** speak.

When the time comes to vote, these citizens will know that they have done all they can to become involved and to make a good choice when they **cast** their **ballot.**

Getting involved as a citizen takes time and effort. Just remember that unless many citizens get involved, some citizens may end up losing some of their rights and freedoms.

Quick Check

Complete each sentence below. Use one of the following words to fill each blank. You may use words more than once.

ballot	civic	donate	involved	preserve
candidates	service	election	enforcement	community

1. People running for public office are known as _____.

2. The city or town in which you live is your _____.

3. To save something is to _____ it.

4. To give something is to _____ it.

5. The police are part of a community's law _____.

6. A _____ group or project is one that helps the community.

7. People who take part in things are people who are _____.

8. An _____ is held to decide which candidates will be voted into office.

9. When people vote in an election, they are said to cast their _____.

10. A club or group that does good things for others is something called a _____ organization.

11. By serving on a jury, citizens are helping _____ the rights of others.

12. Usually voters have a choice of _____ for each office in an election.

13. Planting flowers in a city park is an example of a _____ project volunteers might perform.

14. Obeying the laws is one way citizens are _____ in law enforcement.

15. School clubs and student councils often take part in projects that help the _____.

Review Unit 3

A Choose the word in each set of parentheses that best completes the statement. Underline your answer.

1. A club or group that does good things for individuals or the public is sometimes called a (service, selfish) group.

2. Those who do not treat public property with respect are said to (abuse, cast) their rights.

3. When a citizen acts in a way that could hurt others, he or she may (entitle, endanger) other people.

4. A volunteer is one who (preserves, donates) his or her time.

5. When we try to act as good citizens, we (endanger, respect) the rights of others.

6. A civic project is one that helps the (community, candidate).

7. To take away people's rights is to (donate, deprive) people of their rights.

8. People who take part in making their community a good place in which to live are said to be (entitled, involved).

9. When people vote, they cast a (candidate, ballot).

10. When a person says what he or she thinks about something, that person is expressing an (abuse, opinion).

B Decide whether each example that follows shows good or poor citizenship. Write *Good* or *Poor* in the spaces given.

_____ 1. When Keesha's club sponsored a car wash to raise money to pay for a child's hospital bills, Keesha donated her entire Saturday to help.

_____ 2. Mrs. and Mrs. Nelson did not go to the Meet the Candidates meeting at the high school. "We already know whom we will vote for," said Mrs. Nelson. "We don't want to listen to the others."

_____ 3. Drivers had to slam on the brakes to avoid hitting Sonya as she walked across the street when the "Don't Walk" sign was lit.

_____ 4. Brian called the police when he saw two strangers with flashlights near his neighbor's window.

Facts for Citizens

As we have already discussed, **voting** is both a right and a responsibility. Only citizens may vote. Whether a person becomes a citizen by birth or is a **naturalized citizen** does not matter. Those living in our nation who are not citizens do not have the right to vote in our **elections.**

Any citizen who is 18 years old or older is **eligible** to vote. No citizen may be kept from voting because of race, color, or sex. As you remember, some of the amendments to the Constitution gave these rights to people who were not always allowed to vote.

The first step in getting ready to vote is to **register.** Voter registration is not difficult at all. It means that the citizen who wishes to vote in the next election has to **appear** before **election officials.** These are ordinary people who help other people register to vote.

When you register, you are asked to give your name and address. If there is a question about whether or not you are at least 18, you may be asked to show some **proof** of your age. A driver's license works just fine for this.

Once you have signed your name and answered any questions about where you live and how long you have lived there, you are registered to vote.

In most places, you must register to vote *before* the day of the election. The **county** (or parish) **clerk** or other election officials will **publish** notices in the newspapers telling voters when and where to register. Registration ends about a month before the day of the election. If you do not register in time, you have to wait for the next election in order to vote. In some places, however, you can register on the day you vote.

It used to be that voters had to go to the **courthouse** in order to register. This is not always true anymore. Just before big elections, many cities and counties set up voter registration places in shopping malls, in supermarkets, and at colleges. Recently, a law was passed that said you must be allowed to register where you get your driver's license as well as at other locations. The law also prevents states from removing names from the list because people failed to vote.

Once you are a **registered voter,** you don't need to register again unless you move. Then you do have to give election officials your new address. If you are a woman and get married and change your last name, you will need to notify officials of the change.

If you are registered to vote in the **federal** election for the President and members of Congress, you are most likely also registered to vote in state or city elections.

Voting itself is easy. The list of voting places or **polling** places is printed in the newspaper before an election. You must vote in the polling place that is set up for your neighborhood. If you accidentally go to the wrong place, the election officials will tell you the location of your correct polling place.

Polling places are usually open for at least 12 hours on an election day. The election officials check to see that you are registered. If the election in which you vote uses a **voting machine**, you just pull levers to record your vote. If you use a **punch card** or **written ballot**, you take the card or ballot to a **booth** and mark or punch it to show your choices.

What happens if you know you will be away from home on election day or will be unable to go to the polls because of illness? In most states, you can apply for an absentee ballot. You can have the ballot mailed to you or go to a government office. You receive instructions, a ballot, and an envelope.

To encourage greater voter participation, some states are developing new ways to cast ballots. For example, in Oregon, voters can vote by mail; they do not need to go to the polling places.

A voter checks in with election officials before voting.

Quick Check

Mark each statement below either *True* or *False*.

_____ **1.** Once you register to vote, you never need to register again.

_____ **2.** Only citizens and legal aliens are allowed to vote in our elections.

_____ **3.** If you are registered to vote for members of Congress, you are most likely also registered to vote in city elections.

_____ **4.** The only place to register to vote is at the courthouse.

_____ **5.** In order to get as many people to vote as possible, voters in some places are allowed to register when they go to the polls.

_____ **6.** States now provide for voter registration when citizens apply for their driver's licenses.

_____ **7.** In some states, women are still not allowed to vote in all elections.

_____ **8.** Eighteen-year-olds may now register to vote.

_____ **9.** The only way to find out where to vote is to go to a polling place.

_____ **10.** If a registered voter does not vote for a number of years, he or she may have to register again.

_____ **11.** When a voter moves, he or she has to give his or her new address to election officials.

_____ **12.** If a young voter says he or she is old enough to vote, the election officials do not have the right to ask for some proof of age.

_____ **13.** Some states are finding new ways to encourage voters to vote.

_____ **14.** If you know you will be out of town on election day, you can vote by absentee ballot in most states.

_____ **15.** Everyone must vote on election day at a polling place.

Who Can Run for Public Office?

 Facts for Citizens

When a person decides to try to get elected to **public office,** we say that person is **running** for office. This means that the person who decides to run for office is a **candidate** for that office.

Let's begin by going back to the Constitution. This document gives the qualifications for members of Congress and the President. No one may run for these positions unless he or she meets the qualifications listed in the Constitution.

Members of the **House of Representatives** are elected for two-year **terms.** In order to run for representative, a person must have been a citizen of the United States for at least seven years. Candidates must be at least 25 years old and live in the state and district that elects them to office.

The **requirements** for members of the **Senate** are a bit stiffer. Candidates for the United States Senate are elected for terms that last six years. These people must be at least 30 years old. They, too, must live in the state from which they are elected. Senate candidates must have been citizens for at least nine years.

People running for **President** must have been born as citizens of the United States. These candidates must have lived in the United States at least 14 years. They have to be at least 35 years old. The President's term of office is four years.

What about other **political** offices? Each state has a **governor** and its own group of lawmakers. Remember that the Constitution says that **powers** not given to the **federal government** belong to the states or the people. Each state has its own state constitution. Each state decides for itself what the qualifications will be for the various offices.

In general, citizenship is a basic requirement for state offices. Age requirements vary from state to state. In order to be elected to the state **legislature,** or law-making group, a person has to live in that state.

City and county (or parish) offices have their own requirements. Most towns and cities have a **mayor** and **city council.** Counties and parishes have a variety of elected officials. **Commissioners** help run them. The **treasurer** collects taxes, and the **sheriff** enforces the law. A **county** (or parish) **clerk** is in charge of the bookkeeping and records.

Generally, all these elected officials are citizens and live in the city or county (or parish) that elects them to office. Age requirements vary from place to place.

In case you want to run for public office, there are still more positions from which to choose. Your **school board** is in charge of running the public schools and probably has from five to eleven or more members. Usually any citizen of **legal age** may run for the school board except for teachers who teach in that school **district**. A teacher who teaches in one school district may be on a school board in another town if he or she lives in that town.

 Citizenship at Work
Read about Martha Green. Then mark with an X each of the offices listed to which Ms. Green could probably legally be elected.

Martha Green was born 46 years ago in Los Angeles, California. Her husband died two years ago. Ms. Green has a college degree and teaches in the Los Angeles Public Schools. She has never been convicted of a crime. Her three sons are married.

_____ 1. California state assembly

_____ 2. House of Representatives

_____ 3. Los Angeles city council

_____ 4. Los Angeles public school board

_____ 5. U. S. Senator from California

_____ 6. Governor of California

_____ 7. President of the United States

_____ 8. Mayor of Los Angeles

_____ 9. Los Angeles county board of supervisors

_____ 10. City council of San Francisco

_____ 11. California state senate

_____ 12. California lieutenant governor

Getting Involved in Politics

 Facts for Citizens

You already know the most common way that citizens get involved in **politics**—by voting.

There are many ways for citizens to become involved in politics both before and after an **election** is held. Let's look at a few.

When a citizen decides to run for public office, he or she needs the support of many people. It does little good to run for office unless there are voters willing to help a person get elected.

In **local** elections, such as for a school board, candidates must **petition** to have their names included on the **ballot.** A petition is a paper (actually many papers just alike) that citizens sign. By signing an election petition, the signers are saying that they think the person named on the petition should be allowed to run for office.

If you want to help a local candidate get elected, you can ask people to sign his or her petition. This is called **circulating** the petition.

After your candidate's petition has enough **signatures,** you can be of more help. Perhaps you can take your candidate's **posters** around to stores. These posters give your candidate's name and maybe his or her picture. They ask others to vote for this person in the election.

You can volunteer to work in the candidate's office. You might stuff envelopes, make phone calls, or help schedule the candidate's activities.

Another way to be involved politically is to be part of the group that visits other citizens. Each person visited is asked to vote for the candidate. This is all part of what is called a **political campaign.**

Just before election day, many helpers use the telephone to call voters and remind them of the election. During the same call, they ask the voter to vote for one particular candidate.

On election day, many involved people spend the day helping people get to the **polling place.** They donate their time and cars to drive people to the polls who might not otherwise get out and vote.

How else can citizens get involved in politics? At the time you **register** to vote, you may be asked to which **political party** you belong. You may be a **Democrat,** a **Republican,** a member of a different party, or an **independent.** An independent is someone who does not claim to be in any political party.

Each city or town is divided into **precincts**. There is one polling place for each precinct. Long before state and federal elections, members of each political party meet in each precinct. This meeting is called a **party caucus**. *Caucus* is just another word for *meeting*. Democrats meet at one place and Republicans at another.

It is at these precinct caucuses that people discuss who they want to run for the legislature, for governor, and for President. Even though the precinct caucus is sometimes held in a private home, this is where people who really want to be involved begin their work. These are the people who really have a chance to decide who will run for public office.

Quick Check
One term in the parentheses correctly completes each statement. Underline your answers.

1. For every (city, precinct) there is one polling place.

2. When a person signs his or her name, it is called a (petition, signature).

3. A person running for office takes part in a political (caucus, campaign), which involves convincing people to vote for him or her.

4. A meeting at which party members decide who they would like to run for office is a (campaign, caucus).

5. A paper that citizens sign saying someone should run for office is a (poster, petition).

6. A person who does not claim a political party is called (a Republican, an independent).

7. When you ask people to sign a petition, you are (circulating, registering) the petition.

8. A candidate must petition to have his or her name included on the (ballot, poster).

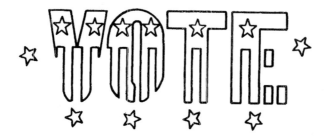

Deciding for Whom to Vote

 Facts for Citizens

The people we elect to govern us have a great deal of control over our lives. They decide what **laws** will be passed, how much we will pay in **taxes,** what **services** citizens will receive, and many other things that affect the way we live.

Since the people we elect to public office have so much power, we want to have the best people possible elected. The question is, of course, how do we tell who is best?

In the last lesson, you learned something about choosing the people who will **represent** you. Not all people want to get involved in a party caucus. Others do not want to take part in a campaign. However, most citizens want to make the best possible choice on election day.

Some people vote for the **party.** A voter who is a Democrat may automatically vote for every Democratic candidate on the ballot. A Republican might do the same. This is known as voting a **straight ticket.** Voters who vote in this manner assume the person chosen by their party is the best person for the job.

Many **politicians** say that a straight ticket is the only way to vote. They feel that everyone elected should be a member of their party.

Most citizens realize that no political party *always* has the best people for the job. These citizens try to become **informed.** They take their rights as citizens seriously. Only after they have learned all they can, do they decide for whom they will vote.

How do citizens learn about the candidates? How does a voter go about deciding who really is the best person for a job?

One of the freedoms given to us by the Bill of Rights is freedom of the press. This allows newspapers to print information. Freedom of the press is extremely important during election campaigns.

Read your local newspapers. For months before elections, the paper will carry articles about the candidates. The candidates will be asked to tell voters how they feel about certain things. They will be asked to talk about important **issues.** The newspaper will report important statements that the candidates make. The paper also tells what candidates say about each other. These things may not always be completely right, but they do give voters ideas to think about.

Newspapers carry what are known as **letters to the editor.** Some papers call this their **readers' forum.** This part of the paper prints letters that citizens write. During election campaigns, voters often learn interesting and valuable things from these letters.

Candidates send out campaign **literature.** Some comes by mail. Some is handed out by volunteers working for their candidate. Take the time to read this campaign literature. Often this material contains facts voters might not otherwise learn.

Groups such as the **League of Women Voters** invite candidates to speak to citizens. Attend these meetings. Listen to what the candidates say. Decide whether or not you want one of these individuals helping make the laws that affect the way you live.

Candidates sometimes **debate** at such meetings. Listen when the candidates are discussing issues. Decide who you would vote for.

Every candidate has important qualifications that make him or her able to do a good job if elected.

 Citizenship at Work
Mark an X before each qualification that would persuade *you* to vote for a candidate.

_____ 1. Experience in government

_____ 2. A college education

_____ 3. Says he or she is interested in keeping taxes low

_____ 4. Married

_____ 5. Over 40 years old

_____ 6. Has business experience

_____ 7. Wealthy

_____ 8. Holds positions with which you agree

_____ 9. Family friend

_____ 10. Volunteers for service projects

Facts for Citizens

Every citizen in the United States is represented by a number of public officials. Here is a quick look at some of the elected officials who help govern all of us.

On the federal level are the President and members of the Senate and House of Representatives. The President **enforces** the laws, and members of Congress are the lawmakers for the entire nation. Any bill passed by Congress and signed by the President becomes law and affects citizens living in all fifty states.

Your state is governed by the state governor and members of the state **legislature.** Nearly all states have both a senate and a house of representatives. The decisions made by your governor and the state legislature affect citizens living in your state. Anyone who visits your state must also obey your state laws.

States are divided into **counties** or **parishes.** Many have three or more **commissioners** who make rules for the people living there.

Cities elect a mayor and a city council to make and enforce the rules by which their city is run. Some cities also hire a **city manager** who takes over the daily chores of running the city. The city manager carries out, or enforces, the laws and ideas of the mayor and city council.

Your public schools are run by a school board or board of education elected by the people. For a great many citizens, the local school board is the group of government officials they know best. This is because most people see education as one of the most important things in the lives of their family members.

States and counties (or parishes) also have other officials who help carry out the task of government. Treasurers are in charge of **finances.** The sheriff enforces laws. The state **attorney general** and the county's (or parish's) **district attorney** work to protect citizens from crime. They may be thought of as the **legal advisors** for the citizens who elect them.

Until citizens really begin to study citizenship, they do not realize just how many people have some control over their lives.

How much money will be spent for the local library? Members of the library **board** help make this decision.

What will the city do for water in the year 2010? This is one of the decisions members of the water board must make.

Citizens living outside of towns and cities in **rural**, or country, areas have other special boards that affect their lives. The fire department has a special board that decides how much equipment to buy.

Members of some boards are elected. Others are appointed by elected officials. All board members and public officials who represent you have important decisions to make about how you live.

Quick Check

Answer each of the following question either *Yes* or *No*.

_____ 1. Do all cities have city managers?

_____ 2. Do the laws passed by Congress affect citizens in every state?

_____ 3. Are members of all boards elected?

_____ 4. Are there always five commissioners for every county or parish?

_____ 5. If you visit another state, do the laws of that state apply to you?

_____ 6. Do board members and officials you do not know make rules that affect your life?

_____ 7. Is your state governed by a governor and legislature?

_____ 8. Does a water board make decisions about what equipment the fire department buys?

_____ 9. Does a bill become a law after the President signs it?

_____ 10. Do your county (or parish) rules affect people living in your community?

What Does Government Do?

 Facts for Citizens

According to our Constitution, the **federal** government is our highest level of government. Laws passed by **Congress** apply to all citizens. Any **powers** not given to the federal government are left for the states and private citizens. This still leaves plenty of room for state and **local** governments.

Here is a short list of what the different levels of government actually do.

FEDERAL GOVERNMENT
- Provides for our national **defense**, which includes the Army, Navy, Air Force, and Marines.

- Handles all **foreign treaties** and agreements with other nations.

- Takes care of **foreign relations**, or how we get along with other nations.

- Makes all our coins and **currency** and sets the value of our money.

- Decides on which items to **tax** and what amount of tax is to be collected on things such as income, gasoline, alcohol, and cigarettes.

- Sets rules for **trade** with foreign nations.

- Regulates the way our **interstate waterways** are used.

- Helps pay for our **interstate highway system.**

- Passes laws that regulate movement of goods and products from state to state, which is known as **interstate commerce.**

- Attempts to protect the civil rights of all citizens.

- Passes laws concerning the safety of **public carriers,** including airlines, buses, and trains.

- Provides a federal justice system that includes the Federal Bureau of Investigation (FBI) and other organizations.

- Builds federal prisons.

- Establishes **national parks** for public use.

- Decides on **farm policies.**

- Sets up federal **agencies** that try to help citizens buy homes, get educational loans, recover from major disasters, and meet other needs.

- Does many more things for all citizens.

STATE GOVERNMENT

- Collects taxes on income, gasoline, alcohol, cigarettes, and other items to help pay for public elementary and secondary schools and state government.

- Establishes and helps support public colleges and universities.

- Builds and keeps up state highways.

- Sets rules and passes laws that apply to the citizens of that state.

- Builds prisons and enforces laws.

- Provides services for its citizens that are not provided by the federal government.

LOCAL GOVERNMENT

- Raises money to pay for services from utility tax, property tax, and license fees.

- Provides for public schools.

- Provides police protection, fire protection, and public medical services. Attempts to maintain a safe city.

- Provides services, such as water and sewage processing.

- Regulates the local government in any area that is not handled by higher levels of government.

Citizenship at Work
Decide whether each item below is done by the federal, state, or local government. Write *Federal, State,* or *Local* on the line.

_____ 1. Sets up the FBI

_____ 2. Operates the highway patrol

_____ 3. Is in charge of the Navy

_____ **4.** Operates Yellowstone National Park

_____ **5.** Manages the United States Mint

_____ **6.** Pays for retirement benefits for military people

_____ **7.** Requires the airlines to inspect their planes for safety

_____ **8.** Collects taxes on property

_____ **9.** Decides on the speed limit on Main Street

_____ **10.** Operates the United States Air Force Academy

_____ **11.** Decides where to build the new high school

_____ **12.** Passes laws taxing Japanese imports

_____ **13.** Decides when to put out a different-looking dime

_____ **14.** Cleans up the city park after a busy July weekend

_____ **15.** Establishes and supports colleges and universities

_____ **16.** Raises taxes to pay for a new school

_____ **17.** Sets the cost of water for your home

_____ **18.** Decides whether private homes or apartments can be built on the next block

_____ **19.** Takes a person to court for a barking dog

_____ **20.** Builds prisons

_____ **21.** Can declare war on another nation

_____ **22.** Makes the choice whether to add a new national holiday

_____ **23.** Tells a business owner he or she has to provide parking spaces for customers

_____ **24.** Inspects public places for fire safety

_____ **25.** Sends an ambulance in response to an accident near your home

Facts for Citizens

The office of President is extremely important. For this reason, the presidential election is quite complicated.

As much as two years before the election, the candidates begin trying to convince citizens that they are the best person for the office. Candidates **announce** that they intend to run for office. Then they and their staff spend months and months trying to get voters to **support** them.

During the late winter and early spring before the election, states begin to have primary elections. In these **primary** elections, the candidates from a **political party** run against each other. At this time they are not running for President. They are running for the chance to run for President.

Late in the summer, the major parties hold their **nominating conventions.** The Democrats and Republicans have separate conventions, which are held at different times. At these conventions, the decision is made about who will represent each party in the November election. Other smaller parties may hold conventions, too.

During the primary elections, each candidate received a certain amount of votes. The more votes a person received, the more votes the candidate has at the nominating convention. The states with the largest **populations** have the largest number of representatives at the convention.

Once each party chooses a candidate, the candidate chooses a running mate, or Vice-President. The **campaign** begins its last few months. It does not end until the day of the November election.

When voters go to the polls on election day, many do not know exactly how they will vote for President. The names of the candidates are on the ballot. The voters vote for the candidate of their choice. However, they are not voting for the candidate. Instead they are voting for people who will vote for President.

This is what is known as the **indirect election** of our President. Each state elects people called presidential **electors.** After the election is over, these people send in their votes. Although they do not meet together, they are called the **electoral college.**

Every state has two senators in Congress. Its number of representatives depends upon the state's population. By adding the number of senators and the number of representatives, we learn how many electors a state has. States with large populations such as New York and California have many electors. States such as Wyoming and Nevada have just a few because of their small populations.

Now we come to the tricky part. The candidate who receives the most **popular** votes in a state receives usually *all* of that state's electoral votes. Popular votes are the votes that citizens cast.

This means that even if a candidate for President receives just one more vote in a state than the other candidates, the one with the most votes gets every one of the electoral votes in that state.

Quick Check
Mark each statement below either *True* or *False*.

_____ 1. Primary elections are held before the nominating conventions.

_____ 2. Only two people are on the November ballot as candidates.

_____ 3. The number of electoral votes a state gets depends upon its population.

_____ 4. Indirect election of the President means voters vote for others who will vote for President.

_____ 5. Votes cast by citizens are electoral votes.

_____ 6. In the state primary elections, members of one party run against other members of the same party.

_____ 7. The candidate who gets the most popular votes in a state usually receives all of that state's electoral votes.

_____ 8. Only the two major political parties can hold conventions.

_____ 9. The presidential electors are called the electoral college.

_____ 10. The candidate who wins the primary election becomes the President.

_____ 11. The candidate for Vice-President is chosen during the primary elections.

_____ 12. Votes cast by the electoral college are electoral votes.

R E V I E W

■ Choose the term from the list that best completes each sentence. Write that word in the space. You will not use all the terms, but you will use some more than once.

election	booth	budget	campaign
candidate	caucus	circulate	city
convention	debate	defense	board members
electoral	federal	foreign	governor
indirect	issues	legislature	local
nominate	party	petition	political
polling	precinct	primary	public
register	senators	signature	straight
taxes	term	trade	voter

_____ 1. A _____ election decides who will run in the November election.

_____ 2. People who are elected or appointed to run schools, libraries, and public service groups are _____.

_____ 3. A voter votes in privacy in a _____.

_____ 4. A citizen who casts a ballot is a _____.

_____ 5. Signing your name is writing your _____.

_____ 6. A _____ is a discussion between or among political candidates.

_____ 7. A Presidential candidate is chosen at a nominating _____.

_____ 8. A _____ is a precinct political meeting to decide on candidates.

_____ 9. To be eligible to vote, a voter must first _____.

_____ 10. People who think much the same way may belong to the same political _____.

_____ 11. Anything that belongs to a country outside the United States is _____.

_____ 12. A lawmaking body is called a _____.

_____ 13. Candidates are supposed to talk about important _____.

_____ 14. _____ are money collected to pay for government services.

_____ 15. To take a petition to people is to _____ it.

_____ 16. Trying to get a candidate elected is part of a _____.

_____ 17. Anyone running for public office is a _____.

_____ 18. City government is _____ government.

_____ 19. A voter who votes for all the candidates of one party votes a _____ ticket.

_____ 20. A person hired to run a local government for the mayor and city council is a _____ manager.

_____ 21. A state's electoral vote is equal to its number of representatives plus its number of _____.

_____ 22. A person's time in office is that person's _____ of office.

_____ 23. Votes are cast for President by the _____ college.

_____ 24. To choose someone to run for office is to _____ him or her.

_____ 25. The national government is known as the _____ government.

_____ 26. The Democrat and Republican organizations are examples of a political _____.

_____ 27. Citizens vote for President in an _____ election.

_____ 28. Citizens usually cast their votes at a _____ place.

_____ 29. You _____ a petition by asking people to sign it.

_____ 30. A state's _____ and legislature make and enforce the state's laws.

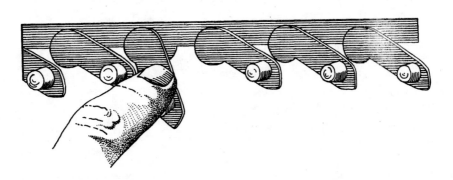

Mid-Book Test

A Mark each statement below either *True* or *False*.

_____ 1. One meaning for citizenship has to do with the way people live.

_____ 2. Citizens have few or no responsibilities.

_____ 3. A Social Security card is a form of identification.

_____ 4. The most common way of acquiring citizenship is by naturalization.

_____ 5. Any person living in a country who is not a citizen of that country is an alien.

_____ 6. School is one of the first places where we get to practice citizenship outside the home.

_____ 7. Rights guaranteed by the United States Constitution are called states' rights.

_____ 8. Federal laws are enacted in the Senate but not in the House of Representatives.

_____ 9. When accused of a crime, citizens have the right to a speedy trial by a jury of their peers.

_____ 10. The highest court in the land is called the Supreme Court.

_____ 11. The Constitution can be changed by adding amendments.

_____ 12. Volunteering your time to help others is one way to get involved as a citizen.

_____ 13. There are no age requirements for those registering to vote.

_____ 14. Few government officials have an influence on our lives.

_____ 15. The President is elected directly by the people.

_____ 16. A citizen 18 or older has the right to vote.

_____ 17. The electoral college elects all senators.

_____ 18. The major political parties choose their presidential candidates at nominating conventions.

B Choose the term from the list that matches each definition. Write the term on the line.

amendments	Constitution	polling places
birth certificate	debate	population
booth	law	primaries
candidates	legislatures	right
community	mayor	treason
Congress	opinion	treaties

_____ 1. Document that proves you were born at a certain time and place

_____ 2. A betrayal of our government

_____ 3. A rule passed by the government

_____ 4. A privilege that belongs to a citizen

_____ 5. The city or town in which you live

_____ 6. People running for office

_____ 7. Elections held before nominating conventions

_____ 8. A discussion among political candidates

_____ 9. The Supreme Law of the Land

_____ 10. The Senate and House of Representatives

_____ 11. What we think about an issue

_____ 12. Locations where people go to vote

_____ 13. Person who runs a city or town

_____ 14. Bodies that make laws

_____ 15. Changes made to the Constitution

_____ 16. Agreements with other nations

_____ 17. Number of people in a given area

_____ 18. Place where a voter votes in privacy

Facts for Citizens

People often think of their government as a group of people who make laws that **limit** or **restrict** what people may do.

Governments at all levels do pass laws that may restrict us. The main purpose of government, however, is to **serve** citizens. Though it does seem at times that some people in government forget the idea of **service,** many things governments do are aimed at helping citizens.

You already have some idea of what things the various levels of government do. Now let's look at some of the services that citizens have come to expect from their government.

We expect our government to protect us. The federal government protects the country's citizens from foreign nations. It also tries to protect us from **criminals** who break federal laws. State and local governments also try to protect citizens from crime within the state and cities.

Protection goes further than just protection from crime. Fire protection comes to mind. How about medical help? **Health Departments** at all levels of government try to prevent the spread of disease. Shots are given free or at low cost to schoolchildren and to the poor so that certain diseases will not develop and spread.

Though private **laboratories** search for disease cures, so do people working for the government. The government also gives money, or **grants,** to universities and private groups to study diseases.

How do we know that we can eat the meat or canned beans from the store without becoming ill? Our government provides for **inspections** to see that food is properly prepared and safe to eat. It sets **standards** for companies to follow so that the food they prepare will be good when we buy it in the store. They also advise us about how to prepare the food so that it is safe to eat.

The government also tries to guard us from taking **medicines** that may harm us. Many tests are needed before a new drug or medicine is allowed to be sold and used for citizens. The long testing process is needed to be sure drugs are safe before many people take them.

Our government tries to provide **housing** for the poor. It sets rules for building houses for others so that homes and apartments will be safe to live in.

Poor people who are sick and cannot afford to pay for medical help have part or all of their doctor and hospital bills paid for by the government. **Food stamps** are given to **low-income** families so that their members have enough to eat.

State and local governments try to keep dangerous drivers off the road. All levels of government help pay for public education. Our entire system of **public transportation** is run by and regulated by government agencies.

In fact, we all receive government services every day of our lives.

Quick Check

Place an X before the services that everyone can expect to receive from the different levels of the government.

_____ 1. Free flu shots

_____ 2. Safe roads

_____ 3. Food stamps if needed

_____ 4. Public transportation

_____ 5. A high school education

_____ 6. Protection in case of a war

_____ 7. A six-room house

_____ 8. Protection from crime

_____ 9. Telephone service

_____ 10. Fire protection

_____ 11. College education

_____ 12. Approval of medicines

_____ 13. Meat inspection

_____ 14. Vacations

_____ 15. Airline transportation

Government Service Programs

 Facts for Citizens

The government has set up many programs to help its citizens. Let's look at some of them.

SOCIAL SECURITY

In the early 1930s, the United States was in the middle of a **depression.** People were out of work, the nation's **economy** was in terrible shape, farmers were not making any money, and many citizens were losing hope.

In 1935, Congress passed the **Social Security Act.** This law was intended to make sure that people who **retired** or who have disabilities would have some sort of income.

Because so many people had no money during the depression, social security made good sense. When a worker reached the age of **retirement,** he or she would be guaranteed some income.

To pay for this income, money is taken out of each paycheck that a worker receives. The worker's employer also pays a certain amount each month for each employee. How much is paid depends upon how much the worker earns. The Social Security payments are a percentage of the worker's total wages or salary.

MEDICARE

In 1965, Congress passed the bill that established **Medicare.** Medicare provides medical payments for retired people.

Just as with Social Security, workers pay into the Medicare fund. Then, when older people have medical bills, Medicare helps pay these bills.

Medicare does not pay all of a person's hospital and doctor bills. Retired citizens have to pay part of the costs of doctor and hospital care themselves. Many retired workers have some money taken out of their Social Security payments to pay for Medicare insurance. Many also buy additional insurance.

AID FOR FARMERS

From time to time, free food is given to people who are already receiving food stamps. Much of this food has been in storage since it was bought from farmers by the government.

Why would the government buy food from farmers? Sometimes the government guarantees that it can sell the farmers' food at a certain price. If the **market** price is lower than that, the government pays the difference.

At other times, the government adds to the price of goods that the farmers produce. If there is no market for the food, then the government buys and stores it. Sometimes the government can sell the food later on. Sometimes it gives the food away.

PUBLIC ASSISTANCE

These programs include public housing, food stamps, and reduced-cost or free medical care. We talked about these programs in Lesson 1 of this unit.

Most public assistance programs are not carried out by just one level of government. Many of these aid programs are run by a combination of all levels of government. Federal, state, and local governments often join forces in an effort to provide a better life for everyone.

When the government makes loans to farmers, students, people starting a new business, and people buying a new home, it is assisting these people, too. The difference is that loans, unlike public assistance, are to be repaid.

Where do the various levels of government get the money to pay for this aid? It comes from **taxes** paid by citizens.

Quick Check
Mark each of the following statements either *True* or *False.*

_____ 1. Medicare came into being as a result of the depression.

_____ 2. Medicare pays all of the doctor and hospital expenses for retired workers.

_____ 3. Since the government pays for Social Security and Medicare, they are free.

_____ 4. Part of the cost of Social Security comes out of a worker's paycheck.

_____ 5. Some students receive government loans to help pay their college expenses.

_____ 6. Only the federal government is involved in providing public assistance.

_____ 7. Sometimes the government buys goods produced by farmers.

_____ 8. The Social Security program was started in the 1980s.

_____ **9.** Public assistance money comes from taxes.

_____ **10.** Workers do not pay into the Medicare fund.

In some states, people receiving public assistance also receive education and training. The idea behind training people who receive public aid is to help them learn job skills.

In the 1980s, some states and counties began what was called a **workfare** program. This program said people who were healthy had to take jobs in order to receive public assistance. The jobs were meant to help the people learn a skill. Once people had the ability to get a job, they would probably leave the program and support themselves. Some of these ideas have worked well; others have not. In the 1990s, Congress passed a welfare reform bill. This bill limits the amount of time someone can be on welfare and who is eligible for welfare.

Citizenship at Work
Decide which of the following ideas are reasonable. Mark those with an X and leave the other ideas blank.

_____ **1.** Nursery and child care needs to be provided when mothers of small children are learning job skills.

_____ **2.** Some people have physical or mental problems that make it impossible for them to hold a job.

_____ **3.** Women who are mothers should never be required to learn job skills, since they have family responsibilities.

_____ **4.** Everyone in the United States should work and should not receive welfare benefits.

_____ **5.** Tax money should not be used to help people in need.

Paying Taxes

 Facts for Citizens

People sometimes say things such as, "It was free. It came from the government."

Nothing is free, even when it comes from the government. Someone has to pay for every service that the government provides. Those who pay for these services are called **taxpayers.**

Let's take a quick look at some of the many kinds of taxes that citizens pay to support their federal, state, and local governments.

One of the best-known taxes is income tax. The federal government and most states collect income taxes. So do some cities. Income tax is paid on the amount of money that a citizen earns. These earnings may come from a job. They may also come from interest on bank accounts or loans. Profits made from a business, from investments, and from selling property are taxable. In fact, just about any money you receive is taxed as income.

Property tax is paid to school districts, cities, counties (or parishes), and some states. This tax is based upon the value of property owned by citizens. Private homes are taxed. So are apartment buildings, businesses, and valuable minerals such as coal.

Sales taxes are paid when citizens buy things. Cities and states collect sales taxes. So do some counties and parishes. From time to time, special sales taxes are collected to pay for things such as transportation improvements. In most places when you buy a car, a skateboard, a book, a CD, a shirt, or just about anything, you pay sales tax on the purchase price. Some places do not collect sales tax on food.

Lodging taxes are collected on hotel and motel bills. These taxes are often quite high in areas where many tourists come. The local citizens feel it is fair to tax people from other places.

When you attend a concert or a sports event, you usually pay an **amusement tax** as part of the price of your ticket.

The federal government and most state governments have taxes on gasoline. Usually these taxes are used to help pay for highways.

Your electric, heating, and telephone bills usually have utility taxes added to the cost of the service you received. These are state and local taxes.

When people buy or sell property, there is a tax collected based on the value of the property.

Travelers pay a special tax on the cost of airline, train, and bus tickets.

Some roads are toll roads. Drivers pay a fee to use these roads. The fee is a form of taxation.

Many local governments issue building permits. Anyone building or repairing a building must display the permit. The cost of the permits varies according to the type of work being done.

When you **license** your car or motorcycle, a part of the cost of the license is tax.

Pet owners pay special **license fees**. Business owners pay for a license to do business. Couples pay for marriage licenses. Drivers pay a fee for their driving license. Those who use state and national parks pay a fee for the right to use the parks.

It may be said that license fees are not taxes. Whether or not they are taxes, they are still paid to the government.

We pay some taxes without realizing it. Every time a **producer** or **manufacturer** pays a tax, that tax is added to the cost of the product. When a citizen buys the finished product, all the taxes paid along the way are now part of the price.

We should not forget **Social Security**. Even though it is called a **contribution**, it is still a form of tax. In fact, Social Security taxes are often the highest taxes that a worker pays.

Citizenship at Work
Listed below are a number of things that citizens normally do. Mark with an X each one that is probably going to result in paying some sort of tax. Leave untaxed activities blank.

_____ 1. Jan bought a new book for school.

_____ 2. Tom went to see the Dolphins play the Giants.

_____ **3.** Diego put ten gallons of gasoline in his new car.

_____ **4.** Mr. Morgan made a thousand dollars profit in the stock market.

_____ **5.** The Browns bought a new home.

_____ **6.** After saving for three years, Mr. and Mrs. Tanaka were able to take a long vacation and stay in a fine resort hotel.

_____ **7.** Bob's monthly salary is $1,200.

_____ **8.** Tim enjoys checking books out of the public library and reading them in his room at night.

_____ **9.** Sara's new car cost her a little over $20,000.

_____ **10.** Bill has to pay for electricity and heat in his new apartment.

_____ **11.** For Mother's Day, Keesha and LeShan treated their mother to a meal in the best restaurant and an evening at a concert.

_____ **12.** Larry's savings account pays interest every three months.

_____ **13.** When the weather is nice, Mrs. Murphy enjoys taking a walk around the block.

_____ **14.** Rosa enjoys making long-distance phone calls to the people she met when she was away at camp. She always calls at night when the rates are lower than during the day.

_____ **15.** Linda tries to add one new tape each month to her tape library.

_____ **16.** Elissa attends religious services with her family each week.

_____ **17.** Kareem donated money to a local charity.

_____ **18.** On her commute to work, Carol Ann pays two tolls.

_____ **19.** Evan pays a cable TV bill that includes a fee collected for his city government.

_____ **20.** The Loverings are remodeling their kitchen and den.

Choose a word from the list below to complete each statement. You will not use all the words in the list.

benefits	Medicare	Social Security
criminals	property	standards
income tax	public housing	taxes
inspection	retired	taxpayers
lodging tax	sales taxes	transportation
manufacturer	services	welfare

1. Those who break the law are _____.

2. Houses, apartments, and business buildings are all _____.

3. Doctor and hospital bills for the elderly are partly paid for by _____.

4. Most things that citizens buy have _____ added to the purchase prices.

5. The cost of federal government services is paid for by _____ citizens pay.

6. Many cities have _____ for poor citizens who cannot afford to pay high rent.

7. Older people who no longer work are _____.

8. _____ is designed to provide some income for citizens who have reached retirement age.

9. When travelers stay in hotels or motels, they usually have to pay a _____.

10. People who pay taxes based on the amount they earn are called _____.

11. Our government sets certain _____ for new drugs.

12. A _____ passes on the cost of taxes paid by changing a higher price for the goods produced.

13. In the 1980s and 1990s, Congress passed bills to reform _____ programs.

14. An _____ is a tax on people's earnings and interest.

Laws and Rules

 Facts for Citizens

We often hear the statement, "**Ignorance** of the law is no excuse." What this means is that, whether or not a citizen understands the law or even knows about the law, the law still applies to the person. This may sound harsh and unfair, but it is the way things are. Since we must live by laws, it is our **duty** as citizens to know all we can about the laws that affect our lives.

Here are some basic rules and laws of which all citizens should be aware:

If a law officer gives you an order, you have to follow that order. If you do not, you may end up being charged with **failure** to obey or even with **obstructing** an officer.

Even if you are not the one who committed a crime, you can get into legal trouble if you are with someone who does something wrong. This is often called guilt by **association**. If you help someone plan or carry out a crime, you are an **accessory** and can go to jail.

If you take something from a store after a fire, flood, or a **riot**, you can be charged with **looting**.

When you and another person plan how to cheat or harm someone, both of you are guilty of **conspiracy**.

When you enter a home or any other property without permission, you may be guilty of **trespassing**.

If you use the telephone to threaten or frighten someone, you have **broken the law.**

If you say things about other people that are not true or that are designed to harm them, you are guilty of **slander.**

A person who prints things that are untrue and intended to hurt someone has committed the crime of **libel.**

Should you buy or even accept stolen things as gifts, you have committed a crime. You are in **possession** of stolen property.

Picking up the phone and calling a place to say there is a bomb in the building is more than a joke. Bomb threats or **hoaxes** are crimes.

No matter how much you resent your neighbors, you may not paint nasty messages on the side of their house. This may be called **malicious mischief.** Riot and **unlawful assembly** are two criminal charges that can be made when a group gets out of control and damages property. If you begin to yell and shout in a public place, you can end up telling a judge why you were **disturbing the peace** or making a public nuisance of yourself.

Armed **robbery** is obviously a crime. However, did you know that if you enter any building intending to do something wrong, you can be charged with **burglary?**

If you physically harm another person, you may be charged with **battery.** Even if you act as if you might hurt someone, or if you threaten to strike a person, you are guilty of **assault.**

If you fail to pay taxes or pay less than you owe, you can be found guilty of **tax evasion.**

What's the answer? It is simple. Be a good citizen, and you will not be guilty of these and other crimes.

Quick Check
Match these terms. Write the correct letter in the blank.

_____ 1. trespassing	a. Planning to cheat someone
_____ 2. accessory	b. Saying harmful things about someone
_____ 3. conspiracy	c. Being on someone's property illegally
_____ 4. slander	d. Physically harming someone
_____ 5. battery	e. Someone who helps plan a crime
_____ 6. tax evasion	f. Printing unfalse statements about someone
_____ 7. riot	g. Not paying all the taxes you owe
_____ 8. unlawful possession	h. Making a public nuisance of yourself
_____ 9. disturbing the peace	i. Keeping or hiding something that has been stolen
_____ 10. libel	j. An uncontrolled group of people who may damage property

Our Legal System Protects Citizens

 Facts for Citizens

You already know that our Bill of Rights goes a long way in protecting the rights of citizens. Over the years, the Supreme Court has often had to decide whether new laws were **constitutional**. Many times our courts and **legal system** have ruled that certain things law officers did were not proper. These legal decisions have helped **safeguard** the rights of all citizens.

Just how does our legal system protect the rights of those accused of crimes?

If you are a **juvenile**, under 18, you may have special rights. One of the most important of these is that you are not supposed to be questioned by law officers unless a parent or an adult **representing** you is present. The idea behind this is that a young person might not understand his or her rights. Having a parent or other adult present helps keep the juvenile from saying or doing things that will harm him or her legally.

Once a person is arrested, he or she must be **charged** with a crime. This means the arrested person must be told what he or she is supposed to have done.

An arrested person does have to give his or her correct name and address. Other than that, he or she does not have to answer questions or give information. This is a right promised by the Constitution.

The courts ruled in the famous *Miranda* case that a person must be told of the right to remain silent before questions are asked.

Under the *Miranda* ruling, an **accused** citizen must also be told of his or her right to a lawyer. Accused persons have to be told that a lawyer will be provided for them if they do not have one or cannot afford one. Also, a citizen arrested for a crime has the right to stop answering questions even if he or she answers some.

You already know that a person who is arrested has the right to let his or her family or lawyer know about the arrest. This does not have to happen the minute the person is arrested.

Once an arrested person is taken to the police station, **booking** usually takes place before the person makes a telephone call. Booking is the legal way of getting a **suspect** ready for jail. It involves such things as giving a name and address. Booking also includes listing a person's property and putting it in a safe place. Fingerprinting and taking photographs may also be a part of booking.

Unless charged with a crime such as murder, most people are allowed out of jail on **bail** to wait for trial. Bail is the amount of money that an accused person owes the court if he or she does not show up for the trial. A lawyer or family member has to **post bond** to guarantee that the accused will appear for trial. Bond is a percentage of bail held by the court as a promise that the accused will attend the trial.

If a citizen is held without being properly charged and bail is not set, he or she can still get out of jail. A lawyer can go to a judge and ask for a **writ of habeas corpus.** This is a legal paper that requires the police to release a suspect or make the proper charges. In many ways, this is one of our most valuable legal protections. Otherwise, an arrested person could be locked up for months or even years and never know why he or she was in jail.

Quick Check
Mark each statement either *True* or *False*.

_____ 1. The *Miranda* rule says a suspect must be told that he or she does not have to answer questions.

_____ 2. The Supreme Court has the power to say that a law violates the constitutional rights of citizens.

_____ 3. A person under arrest has the right to call an attorney or family member within five minutes of being taken to the police station.

_____ 4. Since law officers know what the Constitution and Bill of Rights say, they will never violate a person's rights.

_____ 5. If an accused person is too poor to afford a lawyer, he or she has the right to have one provided.

_____ 6. A person who is arrested must pay the full amount of bail to be released from jail before a trial.

_____ 7. Booking is the process that prepares a person for jail after arrest.

_____ 8. A writ of habeus corpus allows the police to hold someone without charging him or her.

_____ 9. If you are under 18, you have the right to be questioned in the presence of your parents or another adult representing you.

_____ 10. If an arrested person answers any of the questions asked by the police, he or she must answer all of the questions.

Facts for Citizens

Every citizen who is accused of a crime is entitled to a **trial by jury.** This is one of the rights guaranteed by our Constitution and Bill of Rights.

In order to have a jury trial, there must be a jury. It is the responsibility of citizens to serve as members of a jury when asked to do so.

Many citizens know others who have been called for **jury duty,** but have no idea how juries are chosen.

The first step in being selected as a member of a jury starts with a letter in the mail. This letter informs a citizen that he or she is being considered for jury duty. Only registered voters are considered for jury duty. With the letter is a form to be completed and returned to the **jury commissioner.** This person has the responsibility of making certain that there are enough jury members for every jury trial.

The form is simple. It asks for basic information about the citizen. This includes name, address, and place of **employment.** There is also space provided for comments. If there is a reason that a citizen feels he or she should not serve on a jury, this reason should be put in the comment section.

Why shouldn't a person serve on a jury? Mothers with very young children who care for their children at home may ask to be excused until their children are older. Citizens with severe handicaps may ask to be excused. Elderly citizens who would find it difficult to sit in one place hour after hour may also ask to be excused.

The second step in jury selection comes with another letter from the jury commissioner. This letter is a **jury summons.** It is a notification that a person has been selected for jury duty. The summons gives the date, time, and place the citizen is to appear. Some jury summonses give a telephone number to call weekly for a month or longer to find out when the citizen is to report for jury service.

When the person called for jury duty arrives at the **courthouse,** he or she reports to a jury room. There will be a number of other citizens there as well. The jury commissioner or an assistant gives a short talk to explain to these people what to expect in the next few hours. Some courts show a taped presentation that explains how juries work and why we have them.

When **jury selection** is ready to begin, the jurors' names are drawn from a box, one at a time. Those whose names are called are taken to a courtroom. There the **judge** usually gives a short talk explaining how jury **selection** will take place.

The first twelve or so people are seated in the **jury box.** Then the judge and the **defense attorney** and the **prosecuting attorney** ask these people questions. The purpose of the questions is to help the attorneys decide which people seem best suited to be jury members in the case.

Either attorney may ask that a potential jury member be **excused for cause.** This means that the lawyer thinks a certain jury member might not be fair for some reason.

If a jury member has a reason he or she might not be able to give a fair decision, that member is allowed to give that reason. The judge may then excuse that person from the jury.

 Citizenship at Work

Let's look at a few cases involving jury selection. After reading each case, answer the question at the close of the case either Yes or No. Discuss the reasons for your answers with your classmates.

CASE 1
Charles did not want to serve on a jury. He was a carpenter and cabinetmaker with his own business. If Charles had to spend time on a jury, it meant he could not work that day.

"What if I get into a long trial? I could lose a week's work or more," Charles told his friend.

"When I serve on a jury, I still get my regular salary from the supermarket," his friend said.

"Fine," Charles replied. "But I work for myself. If I take time for jury duty, I would receive only the fifteen dollars a day the county pays its jury members. I'm going to write on my form that I'm self-employed. I should not have to lose any money to serve on a jury."

"Good luck," his friend answered.

Will the jury commissioner automatically excuse Charles from this responsibility?   _____

CASE 2
During a three-day trial, jury members were told not to discuss the case with anyone outside the courtroom until the trial was over.

Denise decided to tell her boyfriend what was happening after he promised not to tell anyone else. Her boyfriend kept his word and never told anyone what Denise said to him about the trial.

Should Denise have said anything about the trial? _____

CASE 3

Anna Louise has been selected from the jury pool as a potential juror for a criminal trial. The case involved a traffic accident in which the defendant was charged with driving under the influence of alcohol and negligent driving.

Anna Louise belongs to the organization Mothers Against Drunk Driving (MADD). She also is an emergency room doctor who has worked on many patients involved in traffic accidents.

After the judge and attorneys questioned Anna Louise, they dismissed her as a potential juror.

Should Anna Louise have been allowed to serve on this jury? _____

CASE 4

Alex has received a letter informing him that he is being considered for jury duty. Alex fills out the form, explaining that he has a hearing impairment. He notes that he is able to communicate by sign language and can read lips. Of course, to read lips, Alex must be directly facing the person speaking.

The courthouse where Alex would be serving as a juror does not provide equipment or sign-language translators for hearing-impaired jurors.

Should the jury commissioner excuse Alex from jury duty? _____

Facts for Citizens

You already know many of your rights as a citizen accused of a crime. Many such rights have been upheld by the courts, even though law officers and lawmakers have sometimes tried to take them away.

In the United States, we have what is called **separation of powers.** This is provided for by our Constitution. What separation of powers means is that one **branch** of government has certain powers. Another branch of government has other powers. It is the power of the **judicial,** or court, branch of government to protect the rights of citizens.

Probably the most important right of citizens that the courts have upheld is that all people accused of crimes are **presumed** to be **innocent.** This simply means a citizen is thought to be not guilty unless a trial proves that he or she is guilty. This is very important. In many nations, it is just the opposite. Anyone accused of a crime has to prove he or she is not guilty. This is much harder than having the **prosecution** prove that a person is guilty.

A **public trial** is another extremely important right. At a public trial, family members may attend. So may friends. Sometimes even more importantly, news **reporters** are allowed to sit and listen to trials. If something is going on that is not proper, people other than the accused know about it. With freedom of speech and freedom of the press, anything wrong can be told to others. This helps make trials fair to the person accused.

An accused person has another valuable right. This is the right to force people who have information to come to court and tell what they know. Having a **witness testify** can mean the difference between being proved guilty or not guilty.

Sometimes witnesses do not want to testify. They may be afraid of getting involved. When this happens, an accused person has the right to require witnesses to come to court. This is called the **power of subpoena.** A **subpoena** is a court order that says a witness must appear in court.

Witnesses are supposed to tell the truth. Some do not. However, if a witness is found to have lied in court, he or she has committed **perjury.** The crime of perjury, or **lying under oath,** is very serious. It is so serious that most witnesses tell the truth rather than risk going to jail for lying.

Lawyers may **cross-examine** witnesses. This means the attorneys for the **prosecution** or the **defense** may ask witnesses questions concerning what they have said. In this way, it is possible to discover whether or not a witness has told everything he or she knows. It also helps determine whether a witness may have lied during his or her **testimony.**

Another valuable right of the accused is the right to **appeal.** Even if a citizen is found guilty, that person's lawyers may appeal to a higher court. If they can show that **errors** were made during the trial or that new **evidence** has been discovered, they may ask for a new trial.

Even with all these **safeguards,** innocent people sometimes are convicted. Guilty people are often found to be not guilty and allowed to go free. In spite of these mistakes, our court system is still one of the best in the world. Accused citizens have more rights in our courts than in those of almost any other nation.

Quick Check
One term in parentheses correctly finishes each statement. Underline the correct choice and write it in the space.

1. When a person is called to court to give evidence, that person is asked to

   _____ (testify, presume).

2. The lawyers for the _____ (defense, prosecution) try to show that the person on trial is guilty.

3. In order to require a person to be a witness in a trial, the court can issue a

   _____ (cross-examination, subpoena).

4. In our court system, we assume that a person is _____ (innocent, separation) until proven guilty.

5. If a witness lies under oath, he or she is guilty of _____ (testimony, perjury).

6. Although our judicial system has many _____ (errors, safeguards), guilty people are sometimes found not guilty.

7. If an accused person is found guilty, he or she has the right to _____ (appeal, presume) to a higher court.

8. The person accused of a crime has the right to a _____ (private, public) trial.

9. After a witness testifies, he or she may be _____ (subpoenaed, cross-examined) by attorneys.

10. The accused has the right to require witnesses to appear in court through the

    _____ (power of subpoena, separation of powers).

Facts for Citizens

You have already learned the names of many of the people involved in our legal system. Let's look at the "cast of characters" and see what part each plays in making the law serve citizens.

Police and law enforcement officials try to make the law work. They **enforce** the law. Laws are made by legislators at some level of government. It is up to the courts, or the **judicial system**, to make sure citizens are protected by the laws without losing any of their rights.

Lawyers are **attorneys**. It is their job to **represent** citizens in court. In a criminal case, the **defense attorney** represents the person accused. The **prosecutor** or **prosecuting attorney** represents the **people**. The word *people*, as used here, means "all of **society** or all citizens."

A **district attorney** is elected in each county (or parish). Depending upon its size, there may be a few or many assistant district attorneys to help. It is the job of the district attorney's office to decide who should be charged with a crime.

In major cases, the district attorney has to convince a **grand jury** that there is enough **evidence** for a trial.

Public defenders are lawyers hired to defend citizens who cannot afford their own attorney. These lawyers are appointed by the court to make certain every accused person who wants a lawyer has one.

In court, the **judge** acts in much the same way as a referee at a ball game does. It is the judge's job to make certain the trial is carried on in a proper manner.

The judge not only tries to keep the trial moving but must also be aware of what the law says about certain matters. The judge has to decide whether to **admit to evidence** the documents and items that are presented during the trial. If the judge rules that a document or a display is not proper evidence, then the members of the jury are not supposed to consider those things when they make their decision.

In addition, the judge must decide whether an attorney's questions of a witness are proper or not. The judge also has to decide when the jury should be taken out of the courtroom so that they do not hear certain things.

At times, the judge will have to **rule** on **motions** made by the attorneys. This means the judge has to decide whether a suggestion or request is right or wrong. If the judge makes any errors or mistakes in what he or she allows or does not allow, it may mean a new trial is called for.

Each court has a **bailiff** whose job it is to help the judge by running errands, keeping things in order, and calling witnesses to testify.

A **clerk** helps keep records, answers questions, and provides information for lawyers and other citizens.

In most courts, except **traffic court**, there is a **court reporter** who keeps a record of everything that is said during a trial. This is called a **transcript.** After the trial, this transcript may be used by attorneys when they try to decide whether to ask for a new trial.

 Quick Check
Complete each statement below by filling in the correct word or phrase. Choose your answers from those words or phrases written in bold type on the pages you have just read.

1. Another name for a lawyer is an _____.

2. When attorneys make suggestions or requests during a trial, these are often called _____.

3. The elected official who decides whether or not law officers have enough evidence to bring a person to trial is the _____.

4. A court employee who keeps a written record of everything that is said during a trial is the _____.

5. Officials who try to make certain the law is obeyed are said to be trying to _____ the law.

6. The court official whose job it is to help the judge and to keep things running smoothly is the _____.

7. The attorney who tries to prove that an accused person is innocent is the _____.

8. Lawyers who are hired to defend citizens who cannot afford their own attorney are called _____.

9. The _____ decides whether a district attorney has enough evidence to charge a person with a major crime such as murder.

10. A written record of what is said during a trial is called a _____.

11. The court employee who helps keep records is the _____.

12. If a judge decides a document is something that can be used in a trial as evidence, he or she will _____ that document as evidence.

13. The district attorney or an assistant district attorney appears in court in an attempt to prove the accused is guilty. This attorney is the _____.

14. The person who is supposed to make certain that all rules are followed during a trial and that no mistakes are made is the _____.

15. It is the responsibility of the _____ to make sure citizens are protected by the laws without losing their rights.

16. A judge may rule that documents or displays are not proper _____ in a case.

17. A court reporter may be found in most courts other than a _____.

18. Sometimes a judge must _____ on motions made by the prosecuting and defense attorneys.

19. A prosecuting attorney represents the _____, or all of society.

20. The job of attorneys is to _____ citizens in court.

Facts for Citizens

Among the most important rights we have as citizens are our legal rights. They protect us when we are charged with a **criminal** act. However, not all court cases are criminal cases. Many times citizens find themselves in court for other reasons. These court cases are known as **civil** cases.

A **civil court** holds trials to settle problems between citizens. Courts of this sort may also deal with difficulties between citizens and companies or between two companies.

A case taken to civil court is meant to correct something that is wrong. Sometimes a civil court trial involves keeping something from happening in the future. At times, civil cases involve asking for money to pay for a wrong that has been committed. Payments **awarded** by a court are called **damages.**

If a civil case turns up evidence of criminal acts, then a criminal case may result.

Let's see how a civil court case works.

A car buyer purchased a new car. After driving it for several weeks, she began to have trouble with it. First, the power steering failed. She returned the car to the dealer, and the steering was repaired. Because the car was under **warranty,** there was no charge. However, the owner did have to catch a bus to work for the three days the car was in the shop.

A week later, the lights suddenly went out while the owner was driving home from work. That time the car was in the shop for four days.

Two weeks later, the transmission went out. This time it took over two weeks to make repairs.

During the first eight months she owned her new car, the owner had it in the garage nine times. She had to catch the bus for about forty days in all.

The final straw for the owner came when the electrical system caught fire. The angry owner demanded her money back or a new car. The dealer refused and told her the company would not repair the fire damage.

The owner went to her lawyer, who filed a **civil suit.** This is known as a **complaint.** The complaint asked for $14,000 for the car, $500 for the owner's trouble, and another $200 for bus and cab fares. It also asked that the car dealer pay all **court costs** and attorneys' fees. A jury trial was requested.

The court clerk prepared a **summons** that notified the dealer he was being **sued.** A deputy sheriff **served** the summons on the car dealer. This simply meant the deputy located the dealer, made certain he was the right person, and handed him the court document.

The car dealer had his own lawyer prepare an **answer** to the summons. Both sides in the argument prepared for the upcoming trial.

The main difference between this trial and a criminal trial is that there were no criminal charges. The district attorney was not involved. Even so, both sides involved still had all the rights of a citizen at any trial. This was just a case of one citizen opposing another.

Quick Check
Answer each of the following statements either *True* or *False*.

_____ 1. In a civil trial, the district attorney plays no part.

_____ 2. In civil cases, there is no jury.

_____ 3. Some civil court suits are brought to keep something wrong from taking place in the future.

_____ 4. When people ask for damages in a civil suit, they usually are asking for money.

_____ 5. A summons is often the court's way of letting you know someone has decided to sue you.

_____ 6. The judge helps people fill out the court forms in civil cases.

_____ 7. Civil courts deal only with problems between private citizens.

_____ 8. A civil suit is called an answer.

_____ 9. In a civil case, there are no court costs.

_____ 10. A deputy sheriff usually serves the summons for a civil case.

_____ 11. No one is convicted of a crime in a civil case.

_____ 12. A response to a summons is a complaint.

Review Unit 6

■ Choose the proper word or phrase from the list below to complete each statement. You will not use all the terms.

appeal	cross-examine	juvenile	represent
assault	damages	libel	riot
attorney	defense	looting	safeguard
bail	evidence	*Miranda*	slander
battery	grand jury	obstructing	subpoena
booking	habeas corpus	possession	summons
branch	ignorance	presumed	testify
burglary	innocent	prosecutor	transcript
conspiracy	judge	public	trespassing

1. Taking goods from stores during a riot is called _____.

2. Though it may seem unfair, _____ of the law does not excuse citizens from obeying the law.

3. Because of the _____ case, an officer must inform a suspect of his or her right to remain silent and to have an attorney.

4. A person on trial has the right to _____ witnesses to force them to come to court and tell what they know.

5. To say something untrue that will harm a person is known as

   _____.

6. To threaten to hurt people or frighten them by making them think they will be

   hurt is _____.

7. Another name for a lawyer is _____.

8. A lawyer may _____ a witness after his or her testimony by asking that person questions.

9. The attorney who tries to convince the jury that a person is innocent is the

   _____ attorney.

10. A citizen under legal age is a _____.

11. If someone steals something and gives it to you, you can be charged with _____ of stolen property.

12. In a criminal trial, the district attorney or assistant district attorney acts as the _____ and tries to prove that the person on trial is guilty.

13. In any criminal trial, the person on trial is _____ innocent by the court.

14. It is the duty of the court to _____ the rights of all citizens.

15. If a person is held by the police without being charged with a crime, an attorney may ask a judge for a writ of _____.

16. When a person is notified by the court that he or she is being sued, that person is served with a _____.

17. Witnesses are asked to _____ during a trial.

18. The written record of what is said during a trial is the _____.

19. Civil suits that ask for _____ usually ask for payment of money.

20. The judicial system is one _____ of our government.

21. To enter someone's property without permission may result in being charged with _____.

22. A person who breaks into another's home or business meaning to commit a crime may be charged with _____.

23. When two or more people plan to harm someone or commit a crime, they are guilty of _____.

24. To charge a person with murder, the district attorney must first convince the _____ that there is enough evidence for the charge.

25. During a trial, the _____ tries to make sure no one's rights are violated.

Discrimination

 Facts for Citizens

When we look up **discrimination** and **prejudice** in the dictionary, the meanings of these words seem harmless enough.

We discover that *discrimination* has something to do with a difference in the way things or people are treated. *Prejudice* deals with making a decision that is not based on facts and evidence.

The two words *discrimination* and *prejudice* have been the basis for a great many of the failures in citizenship in our nation throughout our history.

Prejudice is a way of thinking or acting that is based on what people may think is true. This does not mean what they think is *really* true.

The most obvious example of prejudice has to do with race. Based on no scientific evidence, many people assume those of other races to be less smart, less willing to work, and poorer citizens than they are themselves.

The prejudice of some whites against African-American and Hispanic people is a common form of prejudice. However, some African Americans and Hispanics are also prejudiced against whites.

Prejudice based upon religion is also common. For example, some Christians are prejudiced against those of the Jewish, Muslim, or other faiths. Some Jewish people are prejudiced against those who are not Jewish. Some Muslims are prejudiced against non-Muslims. Some Catholics are prejudiced against Protestants, and Protestants against Catholics.

Discrimination is any way of acting that treats one group of people differently from another group. Discrimination often is based upon race, religion, or sex.

It was once common for certain areas in a city to be homes for only those of certain races. When an African-American person tried to move into a "white" section, there was name calling, rock throwing, and worse.

In some parts of the nation, Hispanic people could not hold certain jobs. In some areas, those of certain religions got the best jobs and were the ones elected to public office.

Women have been discriminated against in many ways. Single women could not always get a credit card or a **loan** to buy a house. Women often worked for lower **wages** than did men doing the same job. For much of our history, women were not allowed to vote.

In 1964, the Civil Rights Act became law. In part, it said: *"Employers may not discriminate against any individual because of such individual's race, color, religion, sex, or national origin."*

This law seemed to clear up a lot of problems. However, it caused a new one—**reverse discrimination.** The government required businesses to set up affirmative action programs. These programs recommended that qualified minorities and women be considered first for jobs. Some companies set hiring **quotas.** Through these quotas, companies and organizations would reach racial and sexual **balance.**

This meant that more women and **minority** workers had to be hired and **promoted.** The idea was to make up for past discrimination.

In some cases, white males were not given the jobs or promotions they deserved. Thus, an attempt to right a wrong ended up in making a new wrong called **reverse discrimination.**

 Citizenship at Work
Decide whether the case below is an example of discrimination or reverse discrimination. Write either *Discrimination* or *Reverse* in the blank at the end of the case.

CASE 1

Jerry Murphy had been on the police force for fourteen years. His father had been a police officer, and so had both his uncles. Jerry tried to be a good officer. He worked hard at his job and thought he was fair to everyone he met. Jerry studied hard and passed his sergeant's test sooner than most officers. Then he began to study to become a lieutenant. When Jerry took the test, he finished third in the class.

Because there were to be three promotions to lieutenant, Jerry knew he was going to get the job. When the promotions were announced, Jerry did not get the job. A female officer who finished seventh on the test got the job that Jerry expected.

_____

CASE 2

Cliff was the first member of his African-American family to graduate from college. He held a degree in business administration and then went to graduate school to get an MBA in marketing. After earning his MBA, he worked in the marketing department of a small company.

Five years later, Cliff applied for a position in the marketing department of a major company. He was interviewed by the personnel manager and the vice-president of marketing. Both seemed impressed with Cliff's education and experience. A week after his interview, Cliff received a letter informing him that the position had been filled and advising him that his application would be kept on file. Several months later, Cliff learned that the job had been given to a white male who was a recent college graduate without any work experience.

CASE 3

Estella had been the assistant chef at Gabriel's French Restaurant for four years. When she learned that the head chef was leaving to open his own restaurant, Estella asked the owner for the position of head chef. The owner praised Estella for her excellent skills and talents but told her that he couldn't possibly make her the head chef.

According to the owner, restaurant patrons were always impressed when the head chef visited the tables or made a personal presentation of orders on special occasions. The owner said that the patrons expected the head chef to be a man, and they would not readily accept a woman as head chef. If he made Estella head chef, he might lose business.

Facts for Citizens

Most people know wrong from right. These same citizens have a good idea about what is expected of them in regard to citizenship.

It is too bad that some citizens do not live up to the demands put on good citizens. Some of the failure to make citizenship work as it should comes from carelessness. At times, some citizens are simply lazy. Many times citizenship fails because of **greed.**

One of the terrible failures of citizenship comes from **waste.** For example, waste occurs when aluminum is not collected and recycled. This sort of waste results in use of **energy** and **raw materials** that could better be saved for the future. Waste of this sort results from carelessness or laziness.

Waste in government is another terrible failure of citizenship. This waste costs all taxpayers money. Just as bad is the fact that the wasted money is not spent for the good of the citizens.

Government waste takes many forms. Most are expensive. Most result in cheating citizens by having them either pay for something they do not receive or not receive a service they need.

Some citizens take advantage of the freedoms granted by the Bill of Rights and our Constitution. Every day, some people use the **protection** of freedom of speech to say things that are not true. The falsehoods may hurt others in a number of ways.

In some cases, untrue statements harm the reputations of others. At times, lies cause people to lose time and money.

Freedom of religion is misused by people who want to force other citizens to accept a certain opinion based on religious beliefs. Sometimes freedom of religion is used as a reason for saying that those who do not think and act in a certain way are wrong or do not believe in religion.

Freedom of the press is sometimes misused by some reporters and editors who print things that are not entirely true or are biased. Sometimes this is called **slanting** the news. By misusing the **power of the press,** it is possible to convince others that something that is true is not or that one point of view is better than another.

All forms of crime are citizenship failures. A person who acts in a criminal manner harms other citizens. Such harm takes away their rights as citizens.

Too, citizenship has failed somewhat when citizens cannot settle their problems other than by fighting. Whether the fight involves physical harm or violent words and **accusations,** it is a sign that citizenship is not working as it should.

Nearly all citizens realize that our nation falls short of being as great as it could be. Some citizens work hard at trying to make things better than they are.

In order to make improvements, we already know it is necessary to get involved. For some citizens, this means running for public office. Others work to elect people to office who are qualified to do a good job.

A great many citizens **donate** money to organizations that help citizens who need help. Such an organization is often called a **charity.** Some charities try to help the poor and homeless. Others work to improve opportunities and life for disabled citizens. Many charities specialize in helping citizens with certain conditions or diseases. Some charities work for the members of certain religious groups.

In an effort to improve the lives of others, some citizens volunteer their time and efforts. Volunteers work in hospitals, day care centers, food pantries, shelters for the homeless, and many other places.

Some citizens feel it is their responsibility to spot problems that affect them or others. When they see a problem beginning to develop, they try to call attention to that problem. If the problem is already real, they work toward solving it and changing things for the better.

VOLUNTEERS
OF AMERICA

These citizens use several methods of alerting others to problems. They often begin by writing letters to public officials who can help solve a certain problem. They may telephone officials or meet with them to discuss an important problem.

Letters written to newspapers are another means of calling attention to problems. Such letters let others know of the situation.

Protests and **demonstrations** are other ways of calling attention to problems. Public meetings allow citizens to hear speakers describe what is wrong and what the speakers feel should be changed.

At times, citizens encounter rules or laws that are wrong, but that the courts have not decided are wrong. Sometimes a citizen may find himself or herself with problems over issues such as discrimination or prejudice.

Organizations such as the American Civil Liberties Union and the National Association for the Advancement of Colored People often help such citizens. These organizations provide lawyers for citizens in cases where individual freedoms seem threatened. They also try to get others interested in the problem by holding meetings, talking to newspaper and television reporters, and talking to lawmakers.

The list of ways to help others goes on and on. However, by now you probably already recognize the best way that a citizen can help improve life for all citizens. This is by being a good citizen yourself and thereby setting an example for others.

That is what citizenship involves. Do your best.

Quick Check

Underline the term in parentheses that makes each statement correct. Write that term to complete the sentence.

1. People with a physical problem are said to be _____ (disabled, volunteers).

2. To give money is to _____ (campaign, donate).

3. Organizations that work to help others are sometimes called _____ (charities, demonstrations).

4. Writing letters to newspapers is one way of calling attention to _____ (problems, citizens).

5. People in _____ (public office, food pantries) are often in a good position to help solve problems that affect many citizens.

6. Places where the homeless may stay are called _____ (charities, shelters).

7. A public protest designed to call attention to a problem may be called a _____ (volunteer, demonstration).

8. Those who give their time free to help others are _____ (donations, volunteers).

9. The freedom of peaceful assembly allows citizens with concerns they want to voice to _____ (volunteer, demonstrate).

10. If a citizen needs help because of discrimination, he or she could consider going to a _____ (charity, civil rights organization).

11. Failing to recycle recyclable goods is an example of _____ (greed, waste).

12. Some people misuse the _____ (protection, energy) of freedom of speech to spread falsehoods.

13. Trees are an example of _____ (raw materials, energy).

14. Printing partially true news stories is a misuse of the _____ (power of the press, slanting the news).

Review Unit 7

 Most of the work we have done in this unit has to do with examples of good or poor citizenship. Examples of both kinds of actions are listed below. Write each item in the columns below the list.

1. discrimination
2. demonstrations
3. slanting the news
4. donating money to shelters
5. reverse discrimination
6. recycling
7. saying untrue things about others

8. government waste
9. letters to the editor
10. volunteering
11. protests
12. crime
13. war
14. prejudice

Examples of Good Citizenship

_____

_____

_____

_____

_____

Examples of Poor Citizenship

_____

_____

_____

_____

_____

_____

_____

End-of-Book Test

A Fill in the word that best completes each statement.

1. A person born in another nation who becomes a United States citizen is a

   _____ citizen.

2. Our federal laws are passed by _____ and signed
   by the President.

3. All citizens are guaranteed certain rights and _____
   by our Constitution.

4. In order to hold a job, a citizen must have a Social _____
   number.

5. Membership in a nation is one meaning of _____.

6. A form or paper giving a person's date and place of birth is that person's

   _____.

7. The first ten _____ to the Constitution are known as the
   Bill of Rights.

8. Any person accused of a crime has the right to a trial by _____.

9. The cost of providing government services is largely paid for by

   _____.

10. Our government issues a document called a _____ to citizens
    who wish to travel to other countries.

11. Unless citizens accept the _____ of citizenship, they may lose
    some of the rights they have as citizens.

12. The document that is the basis for our rights and responsibilities as citizens is the

    _____.

13. Before a citizen is able to vote, he or she has to _____ to vote.

14. A person who is running for public office is a _____.

15. A person living in a country where he or she is not a citizen is called an

    _____.

B Mark each statement below either *True* or *False*.

_____ 1. The term of office of a United States senator is six years.

_____ 2. Medicare provides retirement income for older workers.

_____ 3. We elect our President by indirect election.

_____ 4. A person accused of a crime has the right to subpoena witnesses.

_____ 5. A person may be guilty of a crime as an accessory without committing the crime.

_____ 6. Presidential candidates of the major political parties are nominated at national conventions.

_____ 7. Taxes to pay for government services are paid only by those who receive services.

_____ 8. Freedom of speech protects a person from being unfairly sued for slander or libel.

_____ 9. A state has as many presidential electoral votes as it has senators.

_____ 10. Voting is both a right and a responsibility.

_____ 11. A person must be at least 40 to run for Congress.

_____ 12. A total of 11 amendments have been added to the Constitution.

_____ 13. The Sixteenth Amendment made income taxes legal.

_____ 14. The electoral college elects the President of the United States.

_____ 15. A prosecutor is an attorney who defends a person accused of a crime.

C Put an X in front of each freedom or right guaranteed by the Constitution.

1. _____ Freedom of speech

2. _____ Freedom from war

3. _____ Right to pursue happiness

4. _____ Freedom of religion

5. _____ Right to Medicare

6. _____ Freedom of the press

7. _____ Right to a jury trial

8. _____ Freedom from illegal searches and seizures

9. _____ Freedom to assemble

10. _____ Right to Social Security

11. _____ Freedom from want

12. _____ Right to vote

13. _____ Freedom from taxation

14. _____ Right to reasonable fines

15. _____ Right to bail

16. _____ Right to liberty

D Show whether each service below is performed by the federal, state, and/or local government. Write *Federal, State,* and/or *Local.*

_____ 1. Trains the army, navy, and other armed forces

_____ 2. Builds state prisons

_____ 3. Provides Social Security payments to retirees

_____ 4. Inspects restaurants to be sure food is handled properly

_____ 5. Sets up and supports colleges and universities

_____ 6. Provides water to the community

_____ 7. Sends an ambulance in an emergency

_____ 8. Operates the highway patrol

_____ 9. Passes rules for interstate commerce

_____ 10. Provides police protection in communities

**T
E
S
T**

E Write the letter of the tax you would expect to pay in each situation that follows. Choose from the list below.

a. amusement tax   c. lodging tax   e. sales tax

b. income tax   d. property tax   f. utility tax

_____ 1. Juan saved his allowance and bought a new soccer ball.

_____ 2. Mr. Lake owns an apartment building made up of sixteen apartments.

_____ 3. Last summer our family spent an entire week at a beach resort on the Atlantic coast.

_____ 4. For her birthday, Carla's friends took her to dinner at her favorite restaurant.

_____ 5. Mrs. Watson noticed that her electric bill had gone up although she had not used more energy.

_____ 6. Terry's savings account at the bank near her home earns a good rate of interest.

_____ 7. Jason was pleased when his boss gave him a raise in his salary to $500 a week.

_____ 8. Mr. and Mrs. Laing own a three-bedroom house located on the north side of Main Street.

F Write five ways that you can be a good citizen.

1. _____

2. _____

3. _____

4. _____

5. _____